"Allison and Antony have crafted such a joyfu leverage together a love for literature, a love desire to better listen to and honor the voices and lived experiences of the children who grace our classroom spaces."
—Angela Chan Turrou, Co-editor of *Choral Counting & Counting Collections*

"Hintz and Smith have offered a way to ensure that the rigors of mathematical learning and the beauty of literature are attained without sacrificing either. The emphasis on children's thinking, voice, and mathematical wonderings bring literature alive in ways that hold a space for children to learn about themselves and the world. In doing so, they embody the true nature of elementary education at its interdisciplinary best."
—Nancy Frey, San Diego State University

"I love the idea of supporting kids' innate sense of joy and wonder to encourage seeing their world through a math lens. Throughout my life, I never considered myself a 'curious mathematician,' and instead felt quite disconnected, and frankly inadequate, when it came to all-things-involving-math. But 'mathematizing' literature would have been just the thing to pull me in as a kid. Thanks to Allison and Antony, I have a new way of looking at books! I can't wait to use these new skills, and ways of thinking, to encourage the little readers and mathematicians in my life!"
—Gaia Cornwall, Author and Illustrator of the Charlotte Zolotow Honoree and Amazon Best Children's Book of the Year, *Jabari Jumps*

"At its core, this book focuses on the belief that listening to a child's thinking is some of the most important work we do as educators. This book will undoubtedly become a must-have for all primary educators."
—Zak Champagne, Lead Teacher, The Discovery School, Jacksonville Beach, FL

"Grounded in curiosity and wonder, Allison and Antony share ways teachers can engage their students in conversations about texts before, during, and after reading that develop math identities while also bringing literature and math together. The templates included for planning an interactive read-aloud are practical and provide multiple opportunities to invite mathematicians to notice, wonder about, and explore beautifully written text."
—Whitney La Rocca, Co-author of *Patterns of Wonder* and *Patterns of Power*

"**Wow!** I wish every teacher preparation program provided preservice elementary school teachers with a copy of *Mathematizing Children's Literature*. It will inspire everyone to look at math and children's literature in a new way."

—John Schu, Author of *The Gift of Story*

"**Almost a hundred years ago, the great mathematician and educator, Alfred North Whitehead, warned that if we did not pay attention to the stage of Romance, a child's learning would be for naught.** This book will be a valuable and timeless resource for any teacher that believes that the power of children's curiosity, imagination, and identity is rooted in the magical intersection of their literature and mathematics."

—Sunil Singh, Author of *Pi of Life*, *Math Recess*, and *Chasing Rabbits*

"**Joy, wonder, and playfulness exude through the examples of children's mathematical thinking about lovely children's literature selections throughout this book.**"

—Janice Novakowski, District Teacher Consultant & Adjunct Professor

"**KidLit + math = joyful learning!** *Mathematizing Children's Literature* demonstrates how read-alouds provide endless possibilities to explore stories, investigate ideas, and honor children's ability to notice, wonder, and find joy in learning."

—JoEllen McCarthy, Author of *Layers of Learning*

"**Magical.** *Mathematizing Children's Literature* is an organized, practical plan for teachers who want to reveal children's deep mathematical thinking through the books we are already reading in the classroom. Definitely an important book for the modern elementary teacher."

—Theodore Chao, Associate Professor of Mathematics Education at The Ohio State University

"**In this extraordinary gift to teachers, educators Allison Hintz and Antony T. Smith explicitly demonstrate reading exemplary picture books aloud so students notice, question, reason, and discuss as curious mathematicians as well as insightful readers.** *Mathematizing Children's Literature* expertly provides the teaching actions, specific language, and scaffolding you need to champion literacy and mathematical thinking in all young learners. A nurturing, wise, and beautiful book!"

—Regie Routman, Educator and Author of *Literacy Essentials: Engagement, Excellence, and Equity for All Learners*

Mathematizing
Children's Literature

Mathematizing
Children's Literature

Sparking Connections, Joy, and Wonder
Through Read-Alouds and Discussion

Allison Hintz and Antony T. Smith

Stenhouse PUBLISHERS

Portsmouth, New Hampshire

Stenhouse Publishers
www.stenhouse.com

Copyright © 2022 by Allison Hintz and Antony T. Smith

Library of Congress Cataloging-in-Publication Data

Names: Hintz, Allison, author. | Smith, Antony T., author.
Title: Mathematizing children's literature : sparking connections, joy, and
  wonder through read-alouds and discussion / Allison Hintz and Antony T.
  Smith.
Description: Portsmouth, New Hampshire : Stenhouse Publishers, 2021. |
  Includes bibliographical references and index. |
Identifiers: LCCN 2021027495 (print) | LCCN 2021027496 (ebook) | ISBN
  9781625311580 (paperback) | ISBN 9781625311597 (ebook)
Subjects: LCSH: Oral reading. | Mathematics—Study and teaching
  (Elementary) | Reading (Elementary) | Language arts—Correlation with
  content subjects.
Classification: LCC LB1573.5 .H56 2021 (print) | LCC LB1573.5 (ebook) |
  DDC 372.45/2—dc23
LC record available at https://lccn.loc.gov/2021027495
LC ebook record available at https://lccn.loc.gov/2021027496

Cover design, interior design, and typesetting by Cindy Butler
Credits appear on page 211.
Printed in the United States of America
This book is printed on paper certified by third-party standards for sustainably managed forestry.

27 26 25 24 23 22   4371   9 8 7 6 5 4 3 2

For Elham, who showed us the joy of learning mathematics, and for Sheila, who taught us the value of motivating young readers.

CONTENTS

FOREWORD by Christopher Danielson xi

ACKNOWLEDGMENTS xiii

NOTE TO READERS xvii

CHAPTER 1
Celebrating the Joy and Wonder of Children's Thinking 1

CHAPTER 2
Mathematizing Interactive Read-Alouds .15

CHAPTER 3
Book Types and Selection. 29

CHAPTER 4
Open Notice and Wonder Reads. 45

CHAPTER 5
Focused Reads: Story Explore and Math Lens. 69

CHAPTER 6
Idea Investigations: Extending the Read-Aloud Experience. 111

CHAPTER 7
Learning Together as Educators. 155

CHAPTER 8
Family and Community Connections 181

APPENDICES 189

APPENDIX A
Open Notice and Wonder Planning Template 190

APPENDIX B
Questions as Refrain Bookmark 191

APPENDIX C
Focused Read Planning Template 192

APPENDIX D
Idea Investigation Planning Template 194

APPENDIX E
Listening to Students at Work Note-Taking Form 196

PROFESSIONAL RESOURCES AND REFERENCES 197
CHILDREN'S LITERATURE BIBLIOGRAPHY 201
INDEX 203
CREDITS 211

FOREWORD

When I was a child, my father insisted that my sister and I split goodies such as a single donut by the *I cut, you choose* method. One of us would cut the donut; the other would get to choose their piece. This method encourages the cutter to make same-sized pieces so that there is no *larger* piece for the chooser to take.

Many years later, I read an article in a mathematics journal about generalized cake-cutting strategies (Brams, Jones, & Klamler, 2006). My father's favorite donut sharing method was the starting point for the investigation of an increasingly complex set of cases, including that of a slice of chocolate cake being shared by two people—one of whom loves chocolate and one who likes it a little bit. The mathematicians' solution to this problem was to make sure that each person had equal *enjoyment* of the two pieces of cake. The chocolate lover gets lots of enjoyment from even a small piece, while the one who sort of likes chocolate gets a smaller amount of enjoyment from that same piece. The proposed solution is that the chocolate lover should get a smaller piece than the person who likes chocolate a little bit.

This second example of sharing fairly sticks with me because I find the solution absurd. If I only like chocolate a little bit, I probably don't actually want a big piece, while my chocolate-loving friend probably does. Plus, don't I get enjoyment from my friend's pleasure?

Each of these sharing strategies—my father's and the mathematician authors'—is rooted in particular ideas about fairness (which, to the mathematicians' credit, are spelled out with precision in their paper). Also, each is imposed by an outside authority as solutions for how *other* people should share.

I have now read the story of Ms. Burris and her third-grade students reading *The Lion's Share*. Ms. Burris asks her students to consider whether the sharing in the story is fair (spoiler: the students' answer is a resounding *No!*), and whether fair and equal are necessarily the same thing.

Allison Hintz and Tony Smith document a small but satisfying moment in this conversation: Adisa says, "The warthog didn't even want her piece. She's sitting in it!" This is a beautiful response to critiques of school mathematics, such as those from Rochelle Gutiérrez and Francis Su. Gutiérrez (2014) argues that math is too often portrayed as "the highest form of reasoning," and that this status carries with it an "absence of intimacy [and] context." For his part, Su (2020) writes, "Maybe the way for you to see yourself in mathematics is . . . for me to show you that math is intimately tied to being human." When Adisa complains about the warthog sitting on a slice of cake, she is bringing context, her own intimate knowledge of the value of cake, and her humanity to a mathematical question of fairness.

Much of the mathematics that children encounter in school curricula is abstracted for them in advance. The constraints are already imposed by the time the children are invited to touch it. In this important and joyful discussion of a messy story of cake sharing and bad behavior, children are defining their own constraints, building their own abstractions, and creating mathematics as a community.

Allison and Tony's book is full of such examples, and importantly, it is full of concrete strategies for bringing those examples to life in your own classroom, library, or home. They show you how to plan for reading with a math lens, and how to integrate this new practice with your existing read-aloud practices.

As I read *Mathematizing Children's Literature*, I became excited and hopeful for the opportunities these practices will create for children's developing literacy and mathematics. I became excited and hopeful for the mathematicians these children will become—mathematicians who continue our shared work of making the discipline meaningful and useful for broad audiences, inclusive of diverse perspectives, and liberatory for children and all other people. I trust that the time you invest in reading this book and adapting its ideas to your own practice will be equally inspirational for you.

Christopher Danielson
author of *Which One Doesn't Belong?* and *How Many?*

References

Brams, Steven J., Michael A. Jones, and Christian Klamler. 2006. "Better Ways to Cut a Cake." *Notices of the American Mathematical Society* 65 (11): 1314–1321.

Gutiérrez, Rochelle. 2014. "Why 'Getting Real' Requires Being 'Radical' in High Stakes Education." Iris M. Carl Equity Address, given at the Annual Meeting of the National Council of Teachers of Mathematics.

Su, Francis. 2020. *Mathematics for Human Flourishing*. New Haven, CT: Yale University Press.

ACKNOWLEDGMENTS

Six years ago we sat at breakfast with Toby Gordon in Boston (while attending the National Council of Teachers of Mathematics annual conference) to think about the possibilities of this book. Toby, our first editor at Stenhouse and a dear friend, helped us envision and launch this project before she moved into retirement. We are forever grateful to Toby for the ways she listened to our ideas, supported and nudged our thinking, and saw potential in approaching stories as mathematicians. We hope she is finding plenty of time to paint and create as an artist in this next chapter of her life!

When Toby retired, we had the opportunity to work with one of our favorite educators, Kassia Omohundro Wedekind. Kassia brings tremendous knowledge of math education and literacy education. She is humorous, approachable, honest, and a delight to learn alongside. As the editor of this book, Kassia read every chapter draft multiple times. She spurred our thinking, had the courage to say when something wasn't working quite right, and helped us imagine how to move forward when we got stuck. Kassia met with us at every conference, cheered us on, and worked closely with us to finish this book. We can't wait to continue learning with and from Kassia in new ways going forward!

A special thank you to the entire Stenhouse team. The way you lift up writers and support the development and expression of our ideas is phenomenal. Shannon St. Peter, thank you for your careful work with permissions to include children's literature and design work with figures and photos. Susan Geraghty, thank you for guiding us through editing and into production.

We collaboratively developed the ideas in this book with learning partners in elementary schools and community-based settings and organizations. Our learning partners—including teachers, researchers, caregivers, librarians, childcare providers, and parents—have helped shape these ideas through their questions, ideas, and expertise. We give tremendous gratitude to children, families, educators, and staff in Northshore School District, Issaquah School District, Seattle Public Schools, King County Library System, Pierce County Library System, Sno-Isle Libraries, YMCA Powerful Schools, Reach Out and Read, Para los Niños, and Chinese Information Services Center. In classroom settings we experienced engaging discussions and learned alongside skilled and dedicated teachers at Hollywood Hill, Kenmore, and Woodmoor Elementary Schools in the Northshore School District, as well as Lakeridge Elementary School in the Renton School District. Across settings we marveled in the ways children's literature was brought to life through exploration and discussion. You all have been our partners in dreaming up, trying on, growing, testing, and revising these ideas. Learning side by side with you in classroom and family story times has been our most cherished moments of this project! Your playful innovation and thoughtful ideas are all throughout these pages.

Our earliest learning partner was Mie-Mie Wu. Mie-Mie is a children's librarian at the public library next to our university. She knows and finds the best stories! Mie-Mie brings enthusiasm and thoughtfulness to each meeting and every family story time at the library. Her love of children's literature and her inquiry stance to investigating literacy, math, and science ideas add a true sense of adventure to library experiences!

Some of our favorite moments along this journey have been planning for and co-facilitating sessions at math and literacy conferences. Conferences are a time to share ideas-in-progress and engage with, shift, challenge, and grow our understandings in education. Kristin Gray and Erin Gannon have been treasured and playful thought partners in conference sessions focused on mathematizing children's literature. In their roles as a math coach and a literacy coach at the same school, they curated beautiful and engaging stories. They shared stories with students, innovated and experimented with new strategies for reading as mathematicians, listened to students' ideas, and collected students' work. They have been joyful and generous learning partners. In our ongoing work with Kristin, she helped us think about the power of approaching stories with an open notice and wonder as well as a math lens. Our ideas about mathematizing stories, and specifically the different types of read-alouds, have been greatly shaped by Kristin.

This project was supported by our learning partners at Washington STEM, Project INSPIRE at the University of Washington (specifically the Partnership for Early Learning team), the Boeing Foundation, the Goodlad Institute at the University of Washington Bothell, and the University of Washington Bothell Worthington Research Fund. Special thanks to Kellie Holden, who managed to keep us and our many hundreds of children's books organized!

Thank you to our literacy and math colleagues and friends who have greatly informed and inspired our thinking. Some of these educators and researchers include Julie Anderson, Cherry Banks, Diane Barone, Brian Bushart, Tom Carpenter, Courtney Cazden, Zak Champagne, Angela Chan Turrou, Suzanne Chapin, Crystal Kalinec Craig, Christopher Danielson, Andrea English, Annie Fetter, Liz Fennema, Douglas Fisher, Megan Franke,

Nancy Frey, Lynsey Gibbons, Jody Guarino, Cathy Humphreys, Vicki Jacobs, Amanda Jansen, Elham Kazemi, Jenna Laib, Magdalene Lampert, Linda Levi, Kendra Lomax, Ruth Parker, Amy Noelle Parks, Sherry Parrish, Randy Phillipp, Nancy Place, Max Ray-Riek, Regie Routman, Lawrence Sipe, Kersti Tyson, Sheila Valencia, and Tracy Zager.

The educators, many of them mathematicians and math teachers, on Twitter are a constant source of inspiration and our learning community. We learn from their courage to speak up and innovate for a better, more just world for children.

Our families have been a source of inspiration, patience, strength, and love. Becky and Ken, "Mimi and Papa," thank you for giving so much of yourselves to support learning and growing. John and Wilma, thank you for teaching perseverance and determination. Shawn, Grace, William, and Ken, thank you for supporting us as learners. We love walking this life with our families and learning together each day.

NOTE TO READERS

The ideas in this book are meant to inspire your explorations of children's literature—reading aloud, reading together, connecting with children as you explore their ideas, noticings, and wonderings through discussion. We offer these ideas as possibilities and hope they help spark lively discussions, centered on children's ideas about stories, and foster joy and wonder for mathematics among children and adults. There are a few things we'd like to share with you before we dive into the chapters.

First, we hope this book will be useful for a wide range of educators—and although our primary audience is classroom teachers in grades K to three—we think of our work as encompassing parents, caregivers, grandparents, childcare providers, pediatricians, preschool and prekindergarten teachers, librarians, and district-based, university-based, or community-based educators. All of these adults play an important role in children's lives. We often use the word *teacher* to encompass people in all of these educational roles.

Second, throughout this book we use focal stories to think with you about the power and potential for mathematizing children's literature. We hope the focal stories serve as examples within a wide range of children's picture books. The ideas about mathematizing are not bound to these stories; rather, they serve as examples to help us become people who enjoy children's literature and who seek out and find mathematics within any book. Across the time in which we wrote this book, many new stories were published that captured our minds and hearts; today we continue to learn about and explore new works of children's literature. Going forward, we are eager to think beyond fiction to nonfiction, beyond picture books to chapter books, and beyond printed stories to shared family and oral stories. We know from preliminary work with our learning partners that there is great value in mathematizing these different genres and formats, and we look forward to exploring them in future learning with teachers, librarians, and community partners.

Third, we encourage you to delight in children's literature and focus on enjoying the stories! We strive to keep our focus on enjoying and exploring the story, setting, plot, and characters, to appreciate the story the author and illustrator have chosen to share with us. We avoid making read-aloud experiences oral quizzes with specific questions we ask children to answer; instead we notice and wonder, ask questions, and listen to children's ideas.

As you experiment with approaching stories with a mathematical lens, we suggest you begin by inviting children to share what they notice, what they wonder, and what questions they have and follow their lead—placing the child in the center as the mathematician, rather than the teacher always setting the agenda and asking the questions. Think of the story context as a place to play and practice seeing math everywhere in our world, seeing math as a way to make sense of our world. Don't feel pressure to find mathematics in the story, but rather explore as a curious mathematician who asks questions, notices, wonders, and joyfully plays. It can take time and practice to begin to think within a story as mathematicians and also to follow ideas brought up by children to wherever they lead.

Finally, our ideas about approaching children's literature as mathematicians are constantly evolving. We feel these ideas have exciting room to grow, and we are compelled to share them now so that, together, we can continue to learn and build vibrant mathematical experiences for young children, educators, and families through stories. In particular, we are always striving to include in our work children's literature that represents diverse perspectives, a range of life experiences, and themes of equity, multiculturalism, and multilingualism. Our goal is to help children connect ideas in stories to their own lives, so we believe it's important to include a wide range of works from diverse authors and illustrators. We are always looking for additional book titles, and we would love to have you share your ideas and experiences with us. You can use the hashtag #mathematizingchildrensliterature on Twitter. Allison is @allisonhintz124 and Tony is @smithant. We can't wait to hear: What are your favorite stories? What stories inspire mathematical curiosity and wonder? What did your child, or the children you learn with, ask or say during a read-aloud that you found surprising or amazing? What stories deepen and advance our understandings of the knowledge children and families bring to mathematics?

Chapter 1

Celebrating the Joy and Wonder of Children's Thinking

"I notice the diving board is very tall!"
"The people down in the pool look so small from up there."
"I notice Jabari might be scared because he is squeezing his
dad's hand."
"I wonder if he is going to jump."
"The book *is* called *Jabari Jumps!*"
"I agree, I think he is going to jump."

As we listened to children share what they noticed and wondered while reading and discussing *Jabari Jumps* (Cornwall 2017), we were filled with joy. Children shared their ideas with enthusiasm! They noticed details in the illustrations we didn't anticipate. Yes, the diving board *is* so tall that the people down in the pool *do* look really small. The children wondered based on details of the story. Yes, we wonder, too, if Jabari is going to jump even though he feels scared. He *does* seem apprehensive, squeezing his dad's hand while watching other children dive off the high board at the public swimming pool. We were energized to continue thinking about *their* noticings and wonderings.

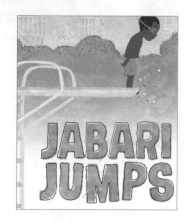

Reading aloud with children is joyful. The surprise of hearing, celebrating, and understanding children's ideas lies at the heart of our work as educators. Although we tend to view reading aloud and exploring children's literature as a time to nurture children as readers and writers, what happens when we think of reading as a time to nurture children—and the adults in their lives—as strong and playful *mathematicians?*

Exploring Children's Literature Mathematically

Exploring children's literature is one of our favorite things to do! From intriguing stories and beautiful illustrations to creative characters and vocabulary, works of children's literature inspire joy and wonder about stories, ideas, and the world around us. Seeing these works from a mathematical perspective makes the experience even better.

The practice of reading aloud is an essential part of literacy instruction, and *interactive read-alouds* are powerful experiences for promoting lively discussion. During an interactive read-aloud, children engage in conversation to construct meaning and explore connections through discussion and shared reading experiences.

In mathematics, constructing meaning and engaging in sensemaking conversation are equally important. Young mathematicians who engage in discussion about their own and their classmates' ideas learn mathematics with understanding and develop more robust identities as mathematicians. In this book we explore what happens when teachers approach interactive read-alouds with a mathematical lens, a process we call *mathematizing* (Fosnot and Dolk 2001). We describe how mathematizing can be a vibrant opportunity to support young mathematicians as well as young readers and writers.

We are both former elementary school teachers in Washington state; Allison worked mostly with fourth- and fifth-grade students and Tony taught across elementary grades. Today, we are colleagues and friends who work together at the University of Washington Bothell, just north of Seattle. We teach courses for students who are becoming elementary school teachers. Tony teaches courses in literacy education, and Allison teaches courses in mathematics education. Through our teaching, and our shared research projects, we work alongside students, teachers, and instructional leaders in elementary schools in the greater Seattle area. We work with classroom teachers as partners in preparing future teachers, holding class sessions with our university students in school and classroom contexts so that our students have opportunities to work with children as they learn about math and literacy instruction. In our research we work alongside a range of educators, from classroom teachers to preschool educators, instructional coaches to children's librarians, families to pediatricians, to explore teaching and learning as well as connections between mathematics and literacy.

In our small university setting, each faculty member has an area of expertise but is also the lone person in our school working in that field. As a result, we tend to collaborate across disciplines. One day, back in 2012, we were chatting (our offices are across the hall from one another), and we started talking about some children's books we really liked. We'd pull children's books from our shelves, asking "Have you read this one?" or "Do you know this author's work?" Or, exclaiming, "Oh! I love this book—look at the illustrations!" Browsing through the pages together, we realized that each of us noticed very different things. Allison said things like, "In this illustration, I notice many children on the playground. I wonder how many children are there? What are all the different ways we could count them?" Tony, meanwhile, said, "I wonder what the children are doing, and I wonder what will happen next!" We realized that we could bring together our research interests around children's literature and reading aloud, a favorite instructional practice of ours and many of our teaching colleagues. We've been exploring, researching, and collaborating about mathematizing children's literature ever since.

Our thinking about mathematizing children's literature has developed over time. When we first began exploring mathematics through literature, we tended to select stories that were overtly mathematical in nature. During this time, we revisited favorite stories we both had in our previous classroom libraries, such as *Each Orange Had 8 Slices: A Counting Book* (Giganti 1999) and *The Greedy Triangle* (Burns 1994). Slowly, we began exploring other stories mathematically, such as *Pete the Cat and His Four Groovy Buttons* (Litwin 2012) and *There Is a Bird on Your Head* (Willems 2007). Our early book lists tended to be mathematical stories. We were learning that mathematical stories can be an exciting and meaningful context to think about, and come to understand, mathematical ideas.

We also learned that although some "mathy" books (especially counting books) can support children to learn important early ideas about number, such as learning and making connections between the numeral, the quantity, and the word (the numeral 3 represents three objects and is written and spoken "three"), the story line may be very limited or not exist at all. Although Allison felt excitement for the ways a counting book could support young mathematicians in learning about number names, quantities, and the counting sequence, Tony struggled to find ways a counting book might support a young reader, especially when some such books had few interesting phrases or words and no storyline to speak of.

Over time, in collaboration with children's librarians and teachers, we broadened our thinking to consider a wider range of stories. We began to ask ourselves, **"What would happen if we approached *any* story with a mathematical lens?"** In what ways might mathematics be represented in a story, even when the story itself might not be inherently mathy? From these experiences three different mathematizing text types began to emerge (and these three types are described in detail in Chapter 3). Our work has continued to evolve, as today we find ourselves wondering, "What happens if we lead with beautiful and interesting stories and use those stories as a context for inviting young children to think as mathematicians and readers?" Furthermore, how might we read and explore a story several times from different perspectives and do so with the goal of listening to and honoring children's thoughts and ideas?

Books like *Last Stop on Market Street* (de la Peña 2015) and *Jabari Jumps* are the kinds of stories we emphasize in our current work and thinking, which has led us to collaboratively design and try out different types of read-alouds for different purposes; we describe and explore these different types of read-alouds in Chapters 4 and 5. We also wonder what kinds of extension experiences might help children deepen their thinking about stories and the mathematical ideas and opportunities they contain. We explore these ideas in Chapter 6.

Teaching and Learning: Our Commitments

In this book we invite you to join us in thinking about how to engage students in lively discussions of children's literature that foster wonder and joy for mathematics *and* literacy. We hope this book will support educators to seek out, discover, and deepen the ways we can integrate literacy and mathematics and nurture robust cross-disciplinary learning for children and teachers. Our primary focus and unwavering concern are children: children's ideas, children's learning, and children's identities as mathematicians and readers. We honor them as people, and we are focused on cultivating their curiosity and learning—their ideas and their identities. This is one of the commitments we have in our work. We'd like to share our list of commitments and describe in more detail how these commitments shape our work mathematizing children's literature and exploring stories mathematically. As you read the commitments we have developed for mathematizing read-alouds, consider which commitments resonate for you. Where do you see some of these commitments reflected in your work? Which commitments would you like to explore further?

Commitments for Teaching and Learning Through Mathematizing Read-Alouds

When we mathematize read-alouds, we are committed to:

1. **Celebrating** the joy and wonder of children's ideas

2. **Expanding** ideas of who gets to ask math questions and broadening ideas about whose mathematics is valued by emphasizing diverse perspectives

3. **Exploring** stories and how they can be a playful context for children to think mathematically

4. **Hearing** children's thinking and listening to understand their reasoning through lively discussion

5. **Providing** opportunities for children to generate their own mathematical questions to explore and problems to solve

6. **Broadening** ideas about stories that empower children to think in mathematically powerful ways

7. **Encouraging** children to make connections between stories, their own lives, and the world around them

8. **Investigating** features of stories to support children's reading, language, and vocabulary development

9. **Supporting** child and educator learning

Exploring Our Commitments

Commitment 1: Celebrating the joy and wonder of children's ideas

We are committed to celebrating the joy and wonder of children's ideas by creating learning experiences that encourage children to think creatively and share their ideas with enthusiasm. Fostering a sense of wonder is vital. As Serafini and Moses state, "A primary goal of education should be developing a sense of wonder so indestructible that it will last throughout one's lifetime. Children's picture books can help foster a sense of wonder and curiosity in young readers" (2014, 466). Children are naturally curious, full of questions and ideas. All children are natural mathematicians who are constantly making sense of their world through mathematics. To pique children's curiosity and spark creative ideas, we understand the importance of choosing rich and interesting stories to explore. The works of children's literature we utilize in interactive read-alouds are interesting conceptually, have vivid colorful illustrations, and provide rich contexts for exploring and discussing all sorts of ideas. For example Elena, a first-grade student exploring *Flashlight* (Boyd 2014), shared her thoughts about a page in the story:

> Oh wow! The beaver on the log is shining the flashlight on the boy! I see circles. I wonder how many there are. I see 1-2-3-4-5-6-7! They are flowers. The moon, and there is a hole in the tree. Ten circles! There's a hole in the paper! And two eyes on the owl, so twelve circles! I notice the grass is pointy like triangles. I wonder how many triangles of grass there are. I would count them in fives or tens because there is a lot. 10, 20, 30, 40, 50, 60, 70, 80! But there might be 100.

She was keeping track of story events while also viewing the illustrations as a mathematician, noticing and wondering interesting details about shape and number and counting.

We also understand the importance of energetic discussions and our role in facilitating such discussions through thoughtful prompts, open-ended questions, engaging talk moves, and honoring children's contributions. By shifting the power dynamic to pursue children's ideas and interests (and not just our own ideas or some children's ideas that seem particularly math-related to us), we show children that we value their ideas and are willing to follow their interests and questions. We hear what children notice and wonder about and explore those ideas, together.

Commitment 2: Expanding ideas of who gets to ask math questions and broadening ideas about whose mathematics is valued by emphasizing diverse perspectives

Children's literature created by diverse groups of authors and illustrators, written from multiple perspectives and about diverse communities, helps us expand our ideas about lived experiences and to see the multifaceted mathematical nature of humans and the world around us. Multicultural stories help us see and learn about ourselves, other people, equity, and humanity. For this reason, our work focuses on narrative rather than informational texts—diverse collections of stories provide rich contexts for exploring settings, characters, communities, and cultures within the familiar narrative structure.

Diverse and multicultural children's literature also helps us expand the idea of what it means to be a mathematician, who is a mathematician, and who is empowered to formulate math questions and to tell math stories. By diversifying the collection of books we read to include a range of stories from a variety of cultures and communities, we communicate that all children are powerful mathematicians.

Commitment 3: Exploring stories and how they can be a playful context for children to think mathematically

Stories take us inside a context where young mathematicians have opportunities to play, to think, and to ask and solve problems with meaning and sense making. A story does not need to be overtly mathematical in nature to be an inspiring mathematical context. For example, *Jabari Jumps* is not an overtly mathy book. Yet, as you saw in the opening of this chapter, children made sense of the story and its illustrations as mathematicians, playfully noticing and counting how many children were in line at the diving board. They curiously wondered about the relationship between the height of the diving board, Jabari's fear of jumping, and the depth of his plunge into the deep end of the pool!

Stories offer a playful context for children to think as mathematicians. Although most curriculum materials include problems that are situated in some sort of context, the complexity of the mathematical thinking those problems afford is typically scant. As we all know, there are plenty of dismal "story" problems that do not reflect the beauty, power, or complexity of mathematics and don't actually contain a story at all! Experiences with these types of problems can discourage young mathematicians from thinking creatively, asking their own questions, and persevering in finding and exploring possible solutions.

In our learning about children's literature as a story context for young mathematicians to reason, our thinking about what makes a powerful mathematical context has been pushed further. We are pressed to consider what is possible in a story context that is different than a story problem. We've come to realize that a story context tends to be more in depth than story problems, and, perhaps most importantly, a work of children's literature doesn't tell a young mathematician what mathematics to be curious about or problem to solve. In a story, there are multiple dimensions that lend themselves to thinking as a mathematician and identifying a wide range of mathematical ideas, concepts, and problems. The characters, setting, plot, and illustrations all provide a multilayered context for mathematics to emerge. A story becomes a play space, and a rehearsal space, for a child to do her own mathematical noticing and wondering, to ask her own questions.

Commitment 4: Hearing children's thinking and listening to understand their reasoning through lively discussion

Celebrating children's ideas means carefully listening to understand them. Few things are more interesting and enlightening than listening to a child's thinking! We are committed to instructional practices that center on children's curiosities and sense making. Sharing and discussing stories is a powerful opportunity to hear what children notice and what they wonder. Through lively discussion, we can hear what children *do* understand and what they are coming to understand. We can design learning opportunities to engage with their ideas and delve more deeply into their questions.

Listening to, understanding, and discussing children's ideas is complex (and joyful) work. Research in math and literacy education helps us understand the importance of teaching and learning through classroom discussions. For example, we must move beyond Initiate-Respond-Evaluate (IRE) patterns of discourse to support students' thinking (Cazden 2001). Discussion is critical for supporting students to reason and learn with understanding (Chapin, O'Connor, and Anderson 2009); it is important to pay close attention to who talks and whose ideas are considered (Cazden 2001) and support students to engage in each other's ideas (Carpenter et al. 2015). Not all discussions have the same goal; facilitating discussions requires purposeful planning (Kazemi and Hintz 2014). Through the examples and vignettes in this book, we invite you to help us build on what educators have come to understand about talk in the classroom and to grow our collective understanding of another dimension of discussion—listening.

As educators, we are called to deepen our listening practices, examining questions such as these: Whom do I listen to? What do I listen for? How do I tend to listen, and what does that listening allow me to hear? How do I tend to respond? Within the context of stories, we can practice opening curricular spaces for children to hear their own and others' ideas, to playfully consider—and grow—their ideas, and to create a listening culture in our classrooms. As Kersti Tyson's (2011) research shows us, children listen the way they are heard.

Through our listening actions as teachers, children learn how to listen to themselves and to one another. When teachers listen to understand—rather than listen for a particular answer—children learn how to listen to understand another. We invite you to join us in committing to improving listening practices in education and planning for and facilitating discussions that support student learning with understanding. How we listen matters for children's learning of mathematics and literacy, as well as for their building of positive dispositions toward the disciplines and each other.

Commitment 5: Providing opportunities for children to generate their own mathematical questions to explore and problems to solve

When we delve into a mathematical world within a story, children have the opportunity to *think up* and *think within* their own questions. What happens when we (teachers or the curriculum) do *not* pose the questions for children to solve? Given space and encouragement, what kinds of questions might a child ask? We are committed to empowering young mathematicians not only to ask questions, but also to know that asking questions is what mathematicians do! We want children to have the cognitive experience of generating the questions our community thinks about and solves, together. When we create opportunities to hear and study children's questions, we can learn more about what is possible when children engage with questions that genuinely intrigue them. We can observe how children are invested in problem solving when pursuing *their own* wonderings and how the space to wonder mathematically may affect their identities and dispositions toward mathematics. We can notice how asking mathematical questions within a story may support asking mathematical questions in a child's world outside the pages of a book.

Commitment 6: Broadening ideas about stories that empower children to think in mathematically powerful ways

The use of stories can empower young mathematicians to think and act in a wide range of mathematically powerful ways. Through discussions before, during, and after a story, mathematicians engage in playful sense making, reason about and make sense of problems, justify their solutions and strategies, listen to and think within their classmates' ideas, persevere through productive struggle, revise their thinking, and collaboratively generate new mathematical ideas. With the story and illustrations as an inspiring backdrop, children engage with meaningful and relevant mathematical content and practices while also experiencing the beauty and joy of mathematics. We encourage children to think more deeply about mathematical concepts and practices, as well as story ideas, through meaningful extension investigations that encourage exploration and creativity of ideas through drawing, writing, using manipulatives, and engaging in role play.

Commitment 7: Encouraging children to make connections between stories, their own lives, and the world around them

Children can be encouraged to connect themes and ideas from stories to events and happenings in their own lives, both in terms of mathematical concepts and in relation to language and story ideas and details. We want children to take up mathematical practices and concepts from stories and notice them in their everyday lives. Once, after reading *City Shapes* (Murray 2016) with a group of young children, one girl looked down at her polka-dot shirt and exclaimed, "Wow! I'm covered with circles!" Exploring the idea of perseverance after reading *The Most Magnificent Thing* (Spires 2014), children shared stories of a time something was not easy for them and when they had to problem solve and stick with it to figure out a solution. The experiences they came up with were amazing, with stories recounted of learning to ride a bike, struggling to make the perfect sandwich, and developing a strategy to play a game in a new way.

Children's literature can serve as a window into the lives of others in places and cultures around the world (Bishop 1990). *Tip Top Cat* (Mader 2014) captures, through vibrant illustrations, scenes of a Parisian neighborhood. *Last Stop on Market Street* takes us inside the lives of CJ and Nana as they ride through San Francisco on a public bus on their way to volunteer at a soup kitchen. *Jabari Jumps* tells the story of a boy and his dad and sister going to the pool, and *Round Is a Tortilla* (Thong 2015) explores shape from a Hispanic culture perspective. Weaving a meaningful thread of multicultural literature enriches our interactive read-aloud experiences and helps all children make meaningful connections between stories and the world around them, from home to their neighborhoods to faraway places.

Commitment 8: Investigating features of stories to support children's reading, language, and vocabulary development

Our work builds on a body of research that shows reading aloud to children "benefits students' syntactic development, vocabulary acquisition, comprehension, fluency, and reading skills such as pronunciation and inflection" (Layne 2015, 8–9). When we read to children, we emphasize response to literature and discussion as part of the experience. This allows children to try out new words, explore ideas from the story, and make connections to their own life experiences. We ask open-ended questions about story events, settings, and characters to carefully listen to children's ideas and to help construct meaning together. We highlight interesting sentences and language structures to encourage children to take up and play with language through engaging conversations. These discussions and activities are grounded in reading aloud quality works of children's literature and exploring them in engaging ways within a print- and language-rich environment for children. Key features of our work reading aloud to children that we will explore throughout the chapters of this book include emphasizing:

- high-quality children's literature

- lively discussion before, during, and after reading

- thoughtful yet flexible stopping points with open-ended prompts and questions

- multiple opportunities for children to share their thinking

- engaging idea investigations to extend children's explorations of language and story ideas after the read-aloud has finished

Commitment 9: Supporting child and educator learning

In our work we aim to support the learning of both children and adults. We acknowledge that the nature of reading aloud, which on the surface is accessible and simple, can quickly become surprisingly complex. We think it's exciting to complexify read-alouds for the purpose of rich mathematical discussion and creative thinking as readers and mathematicians!

We encourage children's learning by implementing a clear instructional routine for mathematizing children's literature through interactive read-alouds. This instructional routine is quick to plan and features before-, during-, and after-reading steps that provide opportunities for prompts, questions, and discussion.

We support teacher learning by working through the steps of the mathematizing instructional routine together. From instructional coaching to co-planning to visiting classrooms and teaching together, our goal is not only to help teachers develop increasingly sophisticated skills in exploring children's literature, listening to children's ideas, and facilitating engaging mathematical discussions, but also to nurture teachers' own identities as mathematicians.

We want readers to feel motivated, encouraged, and safe—to say to themselves, "I know this, it's familiar to me but also exciting and new, and I can *do* this!" We want teachers to be playful with mathematical ideas in children's literature and to try new ways of thinking within the familiar context of stories. We see our work as a safe space for practicing ambitious teaching with instructional moves such as asking open-ended questions and fostering productive struggle. Through stories, we can work on our teaching together as educators and learners, with our own learning (and that of our students) as the focus rather than a curriculum or any particular set of resources.

Across these commitments we hold a vision of rehumanizing mathematics, an action in which we, with "constant vigilance" (Gutiérrez 2018), engage in mathematics teaching and learning that is humane, positive, and powerful for all students. When we hold onto beliefs and practices such as positioning students as sense makers, empowering students to create questions and invent solutions, and encouraging students to seek out joy, connection, and belonging, we are rehumanizing mathematics. In doing so, we honor that humans throughout history have engaged in humane and meaningful mathematics. We intentionally dismantle dehumanizing practices such as the teacher as sole authority and the curriculum as the single source of knowledge, valuing speed and rules over creative thinking, and a narrow view of who is mathematically capable. We create, with students, a more vibrant and inclusive version of mathematics.

Road Map of Remaining Chapters

In this book our goal is to inspire teachers to experience the joy and wonder of exploring children's literature mathematically with children. We hope that by sharing our work, from selecting books to mathematizing them, from facilitating lively discussions and listening to children to collaborating with teachers to learn together, that you, readers, will come to experience the same joy and wonder that we do! Following is a road map of the chapters to come in this book.

Chapter 2 will discuss how this work brings together mathematics and literacy for cross-disciplinary learning. We also overview the mathematizing process of selecting, exploring, and extending children's literature.

We discuss book types and book selection in Chapter 3, exploring questions such as: What makes an engaging read-aloud? Can any book be seen through a mathematical lens? We identify different text types, helping you think about how different books offer different mathematical opportunities.

Chapter 4 takes us inside a particular kind of read-aloud and discussion, Open Notice and Wonder, where children are invited to share what they notice and wonder within a story. This chapter showcases particular works of children's literature and offers planning templates and vignettes to go inside the discussions, together.

In Chapter 5 we discuss two read-aloud discussion structures, Story Explore and Math Lens. This chapter extends the specific examples of children's literature in Chapter 4 and walks you through sketched-in planning templates and vignettes to think about when and how you might plan for these two read-aloud structures.

In Chapter 6 we delve into Idea Investigations, thoughtful extension experiences that deepen children's understanding of concepts explored in the read-aloud and keep them thinking and talking about ideas in stories. From math challenges and child-generated story problems to reading and writing experiences exploring language structures and vocabulary, we consider lots of different ways to extend the joy and wonder of exploring children's literature.

We shift to thinking about educators' learning in Chapter 7, considering what it could look like to learn alongside educators in your context as you study, plan for, enact, and reflect on mathematizing read-alouds. We share some common wonderings we have heard from educators about mathematizing and our ideas about those questions, such as when might the read-aloud occur during a school day and why? Or, how might I plan for a sequence of read-alouds that span a week, a month, or a unit?

We end the book by considering family and community connections in Chapter 8. We think about how to partner with families, children's librarians, childcare providers, and prekindergarten programs to learn together and to make connections between the formal and informal learning settings of a child's life.

An Invitation to Learn Together

We hope you enjoy this book and try out these ideas for yourselves and your students! This is truly the best way to learn. We are reminded of the quote by Deborah Meier that says, "There are, in the end, only two main ways human beings learn, by observing others (directly or vicariously) and by trying things out for themselves. Novices learn from experts and from experience. That's all there is to it. Everything else is in the details" (1995, 181). We invite you to come along beside us as we try out ideas, learn about children's thinking, and consider ways for math and literacy to come together through mathematized read-aloud experiences.

Chapter 2
Mathematizing Interactive Read-Alouds

"Shifting power to students—to make their own meaning and ask their own questions—cultivates a positive mathematical identity and nurtures a sense of curiosity and wonder about the world around them."

—Kristin Gray, Math Educator

"Hearing the words of a text come to life through the teacher's voice is a powerful experience and one that creates engagement and wonder, not to mention endless possibilities for future discussions and thinking."

—Douglas Fisher, Education Professor

Children in Ms. Gray's second-grade class continue to delve into their noticings and wonderings from the story *Jabari Jumps* (Cornwall 2017). Let's listen in as the discussion further examines their ideas.

Asha: I wonder if he is scared because the diving board is really high.

Kala: Look at the picture when he is looking down at the pool *(turning to the illustration that shows Jabari's viewpoint looking down to the pool with his toes curled over the edge of the diving board).* Look how small the people in the pool are!

Malik: They are waaaaay down there *(pointing to the people in the pool).* And he's waaaaay up here *(pointing to Jabari on top of the diving board)!*

Makayla: How high is the board?

Ms. Gray: I hear you wondering about how Jabari feels as he stands on top of the diving board. Asha, you got us started with this interesting wondering. Kala and Malik, you added on by looking at the illustrations to notice that the people in the pool, beneath the board, look really small way down there *(pointing to the pool)* and that Jabari is way up high *(pointing to the board).* Makayla is posing an important question to our

community. She is asking, "How high is the board?" How could
we think about Makayla's question?

Laila: Can you turn to the page where we can see the ladder? *(Ms. Gray flips to pages that show the ladder.)* We can't see all the steps in that illustration. Is there a picture with all the steps?

Zion: There! If you count the steps on the ladder there are 1, 2, 3, 4, 5, 6, 7, 8, 9, 10 steps *(pointing to the steps on the page as he counts).*

Jasmine: How far between each step?

Gabrielle: When I step on a ladder, it is like this *(making an imaginary step in the air).*

Jaylen: Let me measure *(getting a ruler)*! Your steps are about *(holding the stick beside her classmate's raised foot)* . . . Can you hold your foot like that again *(measuring the air distance of an imaginary step)*? . . . About a whole ruler long.

James: So, twelve inches.

Isaiah: Or one foot!

Tiana: Wait, does that mean Jabari is ten feet in the air?

Nevaeh: How high is that *(looking up to the classroom ceiling)*? How high is this ceiling?

Tyson: I would jump from there!

Aki: I would feel scared like Jabari!

Exploring the relationship between the height of a diving board and the emotion of fear is captivating to these children. As they ask questions and reason mathematically about the height of the board—counting rungs on a ladder, measuring the distance between steps, and making connections to their physical space—they begin to see how high Jabari stands with his toes at the edge of the board and why he may feel scared. Approaching children's literature with a mathematical lens, or *mathematizing* (Fosnot and Dolk 2001), is a regular practice in this classroom. Stories are a frequent source of inspiration for children to engage in sense making, reasoning, and problem solving through mathematical discussions of children's literature.

What Is Mathematizing?

Children are naturally curious mathematicians who use mathematics, or *mathematize*, as they make sense of their world. How high is a board? How many steps? How far is a step? We first learned about *mathematizing* from Fosnot and Dolk (2001) who encourage us to see mathematics as *alive*. They write,

> It's questions that drive mathematics. Solving problems and making up new ones is the essence of mathematical life. If mathematics is conceived apart from mathematical life, of course it seems—dead. When mathematics is understood as mathematizing one's world— interpreting, organizing, inquiring about, and constructing meaning with a mathematical lens, it becomes creative and alive. (13)

We are inspired by learning and teaching that is active and alive and grounded in mathematical life—where children and educators create and construct understanding in a community of learners. This speaks to our Commitment 6: *Broadening ideas about stories that empower children to think in mathematically powerful ways.* Mathematizing happens across a child's life—on a neighborhood walk, preparing a meal with family, on the playground with friends. We build on Fosnot and Dolk's ideas about mathematizing to take this practice inside the context of children's literature—to invite children and adults to approach stories as mathematicians, to use mathematics to make sense of the story and bridge the meaning making into a child's lived world.

How Is Mathematizing Stories the Same as and Different from Story Problems?

In Chapter 1 we began to think about how mathematizing stories is similar to and different from story problems. Let's explore this further. The greatest similarity between mathematizing stories and story problems can be found in shared underlying principles and beliefs about teaching and learning through problems, especially the teaching and learning of problems described in Cognitively Guided Instruction (CGI) (Carpenter 1999; Carpenter et al. 2015). Our work with mathematizing children's literature grows out of, and is informed by, CGI. CGI recognizes and celebrates children as mathematical thinkers who have important ideas. Through CGI, we learn that children's thinking lies at the heart of our work and informs the decisions we make as educators.

Mathematizing stories shares a focus on these central tenets of CGI:

- Hearing children's ideas allows us to study and more deeply understand how children think mathematically.

- Children thrive from opportunities to think and reason about different kinds of problems.

- Children solve problems in a variety of ways, and their thinking develops over time.

- Educators elicit children's thinking and engage students with their own and each other's ideas.

- A problem context should be meaningful and relevant to a child's life and empower children mathematically.

In these ways, mathematizing stories is similar to story problems when problems are designed as an opportunity to hear, understand, and support children's thinking as well as to nurture and affirm a child's identity as a mathematician.

There are also distinctions between mathematizing stories and story problems. A stark difference emerges when we examine story problems that are not designed to support sense making or are written in contexts that are irrelevant to a child's life. We have all had experiences with story problems that are uninspiring or even nonsensical. A hilarious and classic example of story problems gone wrong is in *The Phantom Tollbooth* (Juster 1961) when Milo, along with his companion the Humbug, encounters a mathematical character named the Dodecahedron:

> "I'm not very good at problems," admitted Milo.

> "What a shame," sighed the Dodecahedron. "They're so very useful. Why, did you know that if a beaver two feet long with a tail a foot and a half long can build a dam twelve feet high and six feet wide in two days, all you would need to build Boulder Dam is a beaver sixty-eight feet long with a fifty-one foot tail?"

"Where would you find a beaver that big?" grumbled the Humbug as his pencil point snapped.

"I'm sure I don't know," he replied, "but if you did, you'd certainly know what to do with him."

"That's absurd," objected Milo, whose head was spinning from all the numbers and questions.

"That may be true," he acknowledged, "but it's completely accurate, and as long as the answer is right, who cares if the question is wrong? If you want sense, you'll have to make it yourself." (Juster 1961, 174–175)

When a story problem involves a beaver with a 51-foot tail, we agree with Milo, it's "absurd"!

Another difference emerges when we consider who designs and poses problems in a learning community. When mathematizing stories, children share what they notice and wonder within the story context. Through this experience, educators hear and consider children's ideas, and in considering those ideas, children and teachers collaboratively design and pose problems to their learning community. These distinctions of mathematizing stories are grounded in commitments of this work, including Commitment 3: *Exploring stories and how they can be a playful context for children to think mathematically* as well as Commitment 5: *Providing opportunities for children to generate their own mathematical questions to explore and problems to solve.*

Similarly, children take an active role in thinking about what we need to know or understand to study those questions, and they mine the story and illustrations for information that helps us think and solve the problem collaboratively. Therefore, the questions—as well as the information needed to engage with those question—are not put in front of children (as tends to happen with story problems). Instead they must define the problem and identify relevant information needed to examine and solve it. For example, when mathematizing *Jabari Jumps*, children noticed that Jabari was scared to jump, and they wondered how high he stood above the pool on the diving board. To think about the relationship between fear and height, and to figure out how high he was in the air, they posed the question, How high is the board? To think about this problem, they also generated the questions they needed to answer—How many steps up the ladder? How far between is each step?—to figure out the height of the board. Children were powerful mathematical thinkers who generated both the problem and the questions to investigate their problem.

This problem-solving experience is different than a story problem that might read: *A boy climbed ten steps to the top of diving board. There were 12 inches between each step. How high was the diving board?* The problem is defined, and the question is posed—whether or not the question, as the Dodecahedron pointed out, might be the wrong one. The information to solve is given. The purpose is to calculate and get a correct answer (and probably quickly!), not to think mathematically about the world. The power of not posing the question is that children get to be mathematicians who ask and investigate their own questions, rather than struggling like Milo to find an answer (giant beaver) to someone else's question. The power of not giving the information that is needed to solve a problem is that (1) children have the opportunity to think about what we need to ask or understand to study their problems and (2) it avoids problematic solutions and strategies such as looking for and using key words to solve.

How Does Mathematizing Stories Nurture and Affirm a Child's Mathematical Identity and Agency?

How children see themselves—and are seen by others—as mathematicians is significantly shaped by their experiences in classroom and school communities. Through mathematizing, we have the opportunity to nurture and affirm a child's mathematical identity and mathematical agency. Aguirre, Mayfield-Ingram, and Martin define mathematical identity as "the dispositions and deeply held beliefs that students develop about their ability to participate and perform effectively in mathematical contexts and to use mathematics in powerful ways across the contexts of their lives" (2013, 14). The moves we make as teachers send messages to students about who they are as mathematicians and contribute to their beliefs about their ability and belongingness in mathematics. For example, when we amplify a child's mathematical idea and position her competently in front of her classmates, we shape her beliefs about herself (and others' beliefs about her) as a doer of mathematics. In doing so, we nurture and affirm her *mathematical identity*. In the opening vignette, when Ms. Gray says, "Makayla is posing an important question to our community. She is asking, 'How high is the board?' How could we think about Makayla's question?," she is orienting the class to Makayla's thinking. She is communicating to Makayla (and her classmates) that their questions are central to their work as a mathematical community. She is nurturing and affirming Makayla's identity as a mathematician, and she is rehumanizing mathematics by shifting authority from the teacher and the curriculum to the student and valuing students as sense-makers.

When we create space for children to design (or collaboratively design with the teacher) their own mathematical investigations, we emphasize their capacity to make mathematical choices, their mathematical agency. Turner (2003) describes mathematical agency as times when students "identify themselves as powerful mathematical thinkers who construct rigorous mathematical understandings and participate in mathematics in personally and socially meaningful ways" (Turner 2003 as cited in Aguirre, Mayfield-Ingram, and Martin 2013, 16). In the opening vignette, when children posed and collectively investigated their questions, they had *mathematical agency*. These students' ownership of mathematics, as something they do for themselves and as an expression of themselves, is rehumanizing mathematics (Gutiérrez 2018).

We make many decisions when mathematizing stories that matter for bolstering young mathematicians' identities and actualizing their agency, from the selection of stories to the moves we make while reading—and discussing—stories. Throughout, we must think carefully about the characters in the story and the children we teach. To nurture and affirm children's identities as mathematicians and expand views of who engages in meaningful mathematics, we ask:

- How can stories support children and families to see their everyday ways of being mathematical?

- Who is recognized as a mathematician in the stories we read and in our discussions of those stories?

- How can we use stories as a way to broaden perceptions of who has contributed, and is contributing, to making mathematics what it is today?

What Is an Interactive Read-Aloud?

Reading aloud to children is a popular and widespread instructional practice that has multiple benefits. As Regie Routman notes in *Reading Essentials*:

> Reading aloud enables children to hear the rich language of stories and texts they cannot yet read on their own or might never have chosen to read. Our students learn vocabulary, grammar, new information, and how stories and written language work, especially when we talk about the background of the piece of writing and encourage active participation and discussion. Reading aloud—in all grades—has long been viewed as a critical factor in producing successful readers as well as learners who are interested in reading. (2003, 17–18)

Reading aloud is also a fun and enjoyable activity that helps convey to students the positive aspects of being a reader and lifelong literature enthusiast. It aligns well with our Commitment 8: *Investigating features of stories to support children's reading, language, and vocabulary development.* By sharing stories with children, we open up opportunities to help children grow as readers and language users by exposing them to interesting and high-quality children's literature.

When mathematizing stories, we expand this idea of reading to children so that we are also reading *with* children, to incorporate response and lively discussion into the read-aloud routine through the practice of the interactive read-aloud. An interactive read-aloud incorporates children's thoughts and ideas into the experience. Specifically, an interactive read-aloud has seven distinct elements:

1. Choosing high quality children's literature matched to children's developmental, emotional, and social levels

2. Previewing story events and practicing stopping points for discussion

3. Establishing a purpose for reading and focusing upon a small set of concepts, ideas, or strategies to emphasize during the read-aloud

4. Modeling fluent oral reading of the text in the book

5. Using animation and expression to engage children and draw them into the story

6. Discussing the text before, during, and after reading by asking thoughtful questions and pausing during reading for discussion

7. Connecting the read-aloud to extension experiences such as reading, writing, and learning centers. (Fisher et al. 2004, 10–13)

Interactive read-alouds help us address Commitment 4: *Hearing children's thinking and listening to understand their reasoning through lively discussion.* As Lawrence Sipe's research on reader response demonstrates, interactive read-alouds encourage lively discussion and active response among children, who explore ideas in the story and make connections to their own experiences and to other things they know (Sipe 2000, 2002). These experiences also help deepen comprehension. Serafini and Moses (2014) found that discussing book ideas together helps children deepen their understanding of the story, from plot to setting to character traits and motivation. This emphasis on building understanding speaks to our Commitment 7: *Encouraging children to make connections between stories, their own lives, and the world around them.* By exploring and discussing stories together through interactive read-alouds, children are encouraged to make connections in an engaging and meaningful way. For example, when reading and discussing *Jabari Jumps*, children wondered whether Jabari was scared to jump or to even climb the ladder to the diving board. They wondered, how does Jabari feel? Will he ask for help? Will he climb back down the ladder? Children used inference to understand Jabari's feelings, and they predicted what might happen next. Once Jabari *did* jump from the diving board, they sequenced what they saw as a progression of emotions across the story and inferred Jabari's feelings of success and of triumph. Through discussion in response to the story these children actively utilized comprehension strategies to more deeply understand story events and character emotions.

Interactive read-alouds are also a powerful way to explore vocabulary. Graves et al. (2011) demonstrate that reading aloud and discussing children's literature is an excellent way to identify and explore new or unknown vocabulary, including shades of meaning in context. For example, the children reading *Jabari Jumps* considered phrases that hinted at character feelings and what those phrases might mean both in the story and to themselves. They considered the meaning of key words (in bold) in the following phrases, which were familiar to them but seemed to mean something altogether different within the context of the story:

- "I'm a great jumper, so I'm not **scared** at all."

- "I'm just a little **tired**."

- "Sometimes it stops feeling scary and feels a little like a **surprise**."

- "He felt like he was **ready**."

In addition to exploring words and phrases with shades of meaning, Beck and McKeown point out that reading aloud and discussing more complex text than what children could read independently help expose children to sophisticated high-utility as well as discipline-specific vocabulary (2001). We especially pay attention to math-specific vocabulary when it turns up in children's literature with a heavier emphasis on mathematical concepts. We find that such exposure to complex ideas and vocabulary helps children grow as readers and thinkers.

Across literacy skills and strategies we find value in listening to children's thinking and ideas. We see interactive read-alouds as powerful opportunities for formative assessment about children's language use, vocabulary, and comprehension that we use to understand children's skill, strategy, and identify development as readers and to guide instruction to help children continue to develop as skilled and thoughtful readers.

How Does Mathematizing Children's Literature Encourage Cross-Disciplinary Learning?

As elementary school teachers, we often seek out opportunities to integrate the subjects we teach. We also look for more opportunities to infuse literacy and mathematics into our days in formal and informal ways. We have found that interactive read-alouds are a powerful opportunity for engaging students in discussion across literacy ideas and mathematical concepts in a meaningful and integrated way. Mathematizing stories allows us to explore complex concepts and ideas in productive ways to integrate literacy and math and have more literacy and math time in a school day! This seems especially powerful when we find opportunities to approach students' informal mathematical and literacy noticings in everyday moments across the school day.

Within literacy and mathematics, there are shared practices children can work on and learn through interdisciplinary discussion. For example, children need opportunities to learn how to share and explain their ideas or learn how to hear and consider another's idea. Through collaborative conversations of stories, we can explicitly work on these skills that span literacy and mathematics in cross-disciplinary ways instead of in isolation. As we practice what it sounds like to listen across differences, take up and build on or make connections with others' thinking, and ask clarifying questions, children come to see that they can learn and enact these democratic practices as readers and as mathematicians.

Through lively discussions integrating math and literacy perspectives, teachers also have the opportunity to hear what children do understand and what they are coming to understand. We can design learning opportunities to engage with their ideas and delve more deeply into their questions, including exploring stories in an Open Notice and Wonder manner, using a Math Lens, or exploring the story as a reader. These different approaches bring to life the idea of disciplinary literacy—reading text from the perspective of different fields, genres, or areas of expertise (Moje 2007). Stories take us inside a context where children may think and explore as mathematicians and readers, providing opportunities to play and to think, to ask questions and to solve problems with meaning and sense making. We have found that a story does not need to be overtly mathematical in nature to be an inspiring context for thinking, discussing, and learning across math and literacy ideas in an integrated way.

What Is the Mathematizing Process?

Mathematizing children's literature happens in three steps: choosing a text, exploring the text, and extending the text. In the coming chapters, we will take a deep dive into each of these stages. Let's take a quick look at an overview of the process.

Choosing a text

There are many reasons you may select a text. You may select a text because it is a beautiful story that you want to share with students or because the story is important to a student's life inside or outside of school. You may select a text because the story is a good fit with an idea or concept you are studying, or want to study, in your classroom. Or a text may spontaneously become a part of your day—maybe it is brought to you by a student or a colleague or is something you notice on a shelf—and you create the opportunity to share it with students. Choosing a text can be an intentional, well-thought-through decision on your own or with colleagues, and choosing a text can also happen in the moment. All these ways of choosing a text work well with mathematizing.

Exploring the text

Once you've selected the text, you're ready to plan for and facilitate explorations, and discussions, of the text. In this part of the mathematizing process we keep our Commitment 1 in mind: *Celebrating the joy and wonder of children's ideas.* Exploring the text tends to happen in multiple interactive read-alouds over a series of days. We will describe different kinds of reads, including an *Open Notice and Wonder* read-aloud, a *Story Explore* read-aloud, and a *Math Lens* read-aloud. Although these types of interactive read-alouds tend to flow in the order listed here, there is flexibility in order. There is also flexibility in what portion of the story you read or reread. Perhaps you read the entire story once, inviting children to notice and to wonder as they come to know the story context. Then, you may dive back into the book or a portion of the book, or focus upon a single illustration, for further exploration in subsequent reads. As an educator, you choose which order makes sense, which portion to read when, and why.

Extending the text

After sharing the story (often multiple times), you may choose to design an extension experience for students to continue thinking about their questions and ideas that emerged from the story context. We aim for these experiences to be at once challenging and thoughtful, so we call them *Idea Investigations.* This kind of investigation might focus on a mathematical question or wondering anchored in the story, or it might relate to characters' actions or interesting dialogue or vocabulary. Either way, we see Idea Investigations as valuable opportunities to continue the thinking and learning process beyond the last page of the book and beyond response discussions that happen right after a story is finished.

Throughout the mathematizing process we are committed to supporting child and educator learning (Commitment 9) across literacy and mathematics in an integrated way. In this process we celebrate the joy of exploring children's literature from different perspectives, taking care to listen to children's ideas, to pause and ponder ideas that we find intriguing or puzzling, to ask questions, and to wonder about the world. We invite you to join us in this process.

Reflection and Discussion Questions

As you finish reading this chapter, here are some reflection questions for you to consider on your own or with colleagues:

1. Why do we pose story problems? What is their purpose, and how might discussion of students' ideas while reading children's literature achieve the same purpose?

2. In my own words, what is a mathematical identity? How do I nurture and affirm a child's identity as a mathematician? In my own words, what is mathematical agency? How do I nurture and affirm students' agency as mathematicians?

3. Which aspects of deepening cross-disciplinary learning through mathematizing children's literature are the most inspiring to me? Why?

Chapter 3
Book Types and Selection

> Choosing a book to read aloud depends upon
> a variety of factors, but perhaps first and foremost a
> read-aloud should spark children's interest.
>
> —Mie-Mie Wu, Children's Librarian

One memorable day, our research partner Mie-Mie Wu, the children's librarian at the public library near our university, rolled cartloads of books into our meeting so we could think more about mathematizing stories. There were nearly 400 children's literature titles on those carts spanning classics to new publications! With the books spread out across tables and teetering in stacks, we asked ourselves, "Can *any* book be seen through a mathematical lens?"

Mie-Mie had preselected the books based on her knowledge of choosing stories for reading aloud with children and their families. She is an expert at finding and selecting stories that make an engaging read-aloud. You should see her bring a book to life as she engages children and adults in a read-aloud (Figure 3.1)—especially when she wears her vibrant pajamas to evening story time! She explained to us,

> It almost goes without saying that if a reader has enthusiasm for the story, then that excitement and interest will carry over in the delivery, presentation, and dynamic act of reading aloud and together. In turn, a lively reading can motivate an audience to interact with a story in unanticipated ways, furthering opportunities to explore, discuss, and engage with the text.

Mie-Mie's ideas about what makes an engaging read-aloud stem from her work as a children's librarian. She is inspired by books such as *The Read-Aloud Handbook* by Jim Trelease (2013), *How to Get Your Child to Love Reading* by Esme Raji Codell (2003), and *In Defense of Read-Aloud: Sustaining Best Practice* by Steven Layne (2015). From these authors we learn that, although every reader and audience is unique, certain characteristics have widespread appeal for readers and listeners alike. Here is a list of these characteristics:

Figure 3.1
Mie-Mie Reading Aloud
at Children's Story Time in the Public Library

Children's Literature Read-Aloud Characteristics

- **Hook**—What instantly attracts children's attention? A beguiling first sentence? A funny word or title? An opening picture or sequence that begs for a story or explanation? Is there a problem to be solved?

- **Humor**—How might we encourage laughter throughout the reading? Is there a silly premise, funny plot, or hilarious words or characters to encourage laughter?

- **Emphasis**—Are there characters, actions, feelings, or elements of the plot that can be emphasized when reading aloud? Do they lend themselves to dramatic pause or stopping points?

- **Narrative pacing**—Does the story have predictability or a twist ending? Is there a pattern to the telling of the story or aspects of a cumulative tale? Do parts of the story happen very quickly, or do they unfold more slowly and deliberately?

- **Literary style**—What is the mood, atmosphere, or tone of the text? How do the author's choices in diction, vocabulary, and narrative shape the style of the story and reading experience? Is the story conversational, pert, or interactive, or is it quiet, contemplative, or expansive?

- **Visual interest**—What is the artistic quality of illustrations in the text? How might illustrations help enhance the story experience? What do students notice in illustrations, and how do the illustrations help them predict what might happen next? How do the illustrations support or contrast with the text in the story?

- **Audience participation**—How might we invite students to join in the storytelling? Is there a repeated phrase or action to boost participation?

- **Engaging Experience**—What are the students' experiences in encountering the story as a whole? What do they feel in hearing and seeing the story and how do they choose to engage with it? What are they interested in further exploring?

Let's go back to that moment when Mie-Mie wheeled in the carts of books. Drawing upon Mie-Mie's knowledge, we began this stage of the book-selection process with the idea that these books could lend themselves to an engaging read-aloud. This was an important start because we want to select stories that inspire children so that we can hear and play with *their* ideas through lively discussion. We shared laughs about the differences in what we paid attention to as we approached stories, and together we expanded what we each valued in selecting books. Tony continued to help Allison appreciate the story line and the feelings of the characters. Allison noticed how Tony laughed aloud with joy while reading or when he enthusiastically pointed out clever words or details in the illustrations. Allison helped Tony identify and think about mathematical content and practices in story ideas and illustrations, from number groupings to shape to perspective to perseverance. Mie-Mie kept us both focused on read-aloud characteristics, especially visual interest and potential audience participation. Slowly, we began to identify stories we collectively believed had three essential features: meeting the read-aloud characteristics above, possessing interesting literary features, and creating rich potential for mathematical inquiry.

Three Book Types

After we identified stories that we believed met all three of the characteristics, another dimension of noticings emerged. We began paying attention to the different ways that mathematics was, or was not, central to the story or the illustrations. We noticed that in some stories, the plot was mathematical, and in others, there was mathematical potential, and sometimes it was interesting to glance at an illustration for a moment with a mathematical eye. From this experience, three overlapping categories of book types began to take shape.

One category was a teetering pile of "mathy" books. These were the books where mathematics was central to the story—mathematics is a part of the plot and is intertwined with the problem and resolution of the story. We began calling these *text-dependent* books—those that point readers to think in a mathematical way and where it would be challenging to read and understand the story without thinking mathematically. An example of a text-dependent book is *Splash!* (Jonas 1997). This story takes place by a backyard pond where animals, such as turtles, frogs, and a dog, jump into and out of the pond, and other animals, such as catfish and goldfish, swim in the pond.  Other creatures come and go, including a dragonfly, a robin, a girl, and even a house cat that ends up in the pond, much to its dismay! With each turning page, the number of animals in the pond changes, and the reader is asked, "How many are in my pond?" A reader can count the animals by ones or, as we heard children do, pay attention to how the numbers change from page to page and think relationally about quantities. The stories in this stack, like *Splash!,* are overtly and inherently mathematical.

A second pile was brimming with books that had mathematical potential, but where the mathematics was not central to story events or plot. In this type of book, a reader could enjoy the story and not pay attention to the mathematics at all, or, if one did notice and think about the mathematics, it could deepen understanding of the story. We began calling these *idea-enhancing* books. *The Rainbow Fish* (Pfister 1992), a well-known children's story, is an idea-enhancing book. We wondered, for example, what might children notice and wonder about the rainbow fish's magical scales and the quantity of scales it shared with its friends if they approached this story with a mathematical lens? Listening to children's noticings and wonderings, we heard that children were thinking about quantity in relation to the themes of generosity and friendship in many different ways! Considering this story mathematically helped children understand these themes more deeply.

Finally, a third pile of books was growing. In these books mathematics was not central to the story, nor did the story lend itself strongly to mathematizing, yet there were brief moments in the pictures or words where one may pause to think mathematically. We began calling these *illustration-exploring* books. *Grumpy Bird* (Tankard 2007) is an illustration-exploring book. In this story, Bird stomps along on a walk, encountering animal friends who decide to follow along. Although the story itself does not mention the number of friends, several illustrations provide opportunities to see combinations of six in different ways. Additionally, a few illustrations show all five friends plus Bird but, due to perspective and placing, do not show all the legs of each animal. This provides an opportunity to narrow upon the illustration and pose questions about how many legs there are altogether and how students are counting.

Sometimes a book can fall into more than one category. For example, with *Grumpy Bird* we had experiences where children explored the illustrations mathematically, and then when we listened to their mathematical ideas, our thinking changed in response to what students were noticing and wondering about. In this case, students noticed Bird, though grumpy, ended up with quite a few friends following along on his walk. Quantifying this noticing (how many friends) added to the story, causing the book to fall into the idea-enhancing category as well as the illustration-exploring category. This kind of experience tells us that these three book categories overlap along a continuum and are not entirely separate.

Although it is not important to be able to cleanly categorize books as one text type or another, it can be helpful to know that the degree to which mathematics is central to, or available in, a story varies and that different books lend themselves to different mathematical opportunities, experiences, and purposes. Also, that nearly *every* story has mathematical potential!

Text-dependent books

There is a small bookstore in Seattle, the city where we live, that is a mathematical wonderland. It is an old house, painted pale yellow, that is warm, inviting, and full of inspiration when you walk inside. Within this store, one of our favorite sections is a colorful book area that is well stocked with mathy books! Organized by mathematical domains, you can enjoy picture books and chapter books about everything from counting to geometry to the history of mathematics. If you're looking for a book that is mathematical in theme or has mathematics integrated with the plot of a story, you'll find it within these shelves and bins. As we thumb through these books, we find joy in the stories.

Full House: An Invitation to Fractions (Dodds 2009) is an example text-dependent book that takes you inside the Strawberry Inn where Miss Bloom welcomes guests to stay and join her for dinner. The characters are silly, there is singsong rhyming text, and the illustrations are whimsical. Readers are invited to think about fractions in two different ways—one is the way the inn rooms are filled and the other is the way the characters divide a midnight snack.

The Strawberry Inn has six rooms, one of which is where Miss Bloom lives. As the guests arrive, one by one, one sixth of the inn is filled. There is a fraction notation at the bottom of the page to show how many rooms are full. For example, when the first guest, Sea Captain Duffy, arrives and checks into room number one, the story reads, "One room of six had a guest for the night," and the fraction $\frac{1}{6}$ is shown. And when the second guest arrives, the Duchess Boofaye (and her dog Smoochie), "two rooms of six" have guests and $\frac{2}{6}$ is shown. This pattern continues until all five of the guests have checked in and the inn is full (remember, Miss Bloom lives in one of the six rooms). After eating dinner together and saying goodnight, Miss Bloom discovers that all the guests have sneaked down to the kitchen to share a cake!

Fractions are central to the story of *Full House*. The plot depends on thinking about how each room is a portion of the inn, when the inn is full, and what portion of a cake each guest gets to eat. There is mathematical language, such as "two rooms of six" and "thank you for saving the last piece for me." There are mathematical notations, such as a fraction on each page as the inn is filled, and a representation of the cake cut into sixths with $\frac{6}{6} = 1$. From the title of the book, to the ideas in the story, to the mathematical symbols, this story is overtly mathematical. We would really miss something about this story if we did not have the chance to make sense of fractions. For this reason, we think of stories such as *Full House* as text-dependent books.

Another text-dependent book that captivated us is *Square Cat* (Schoonmaker 2011). This is a story about a cat that struggles with her identity and is ultimately helped in finding happiness by her two loyal friends. In this heartwarming tale, we connect with Eula, the "square cat living in a round world," and we learn why life isn't easy when you're square. For example, it is a problem when Eula repeatedly tips over. What is it about being square that makes it hard to get back up? Eula's friends, Patsy and Maude, who are both round cats, try to lift her spirits by giving her round things—hoop earrings, donuts, and red rouge circles on her cheeks—but ultimately, it is their slipping into a box and becoming square, too, that brings Eula's purr back. In this story, the central problem is geometrical; the features of a square are not fitting of a feline that ought to be round! Understanding concepts of shape are essential to comprehending the story.

These kinds of text-dependent stories manage to balance mathematical ideas with an engaging and entertaining story. In our experience this kind of balance creates opportunities for children to explore ideas within a story, pose questions and mathematical problems, and engage in discussion about their thinking. We have found that sometimes this balance is hard to find, especially with counting books. Without a plot, interesting story events, or compelling characters, a typical counting book might end up as a simple number sequence. More creative and compelling counting books incorporate interesting story elements into the sequence. *Dog's Colorful Day* (Dodd 2003) is an example, as it combines counting one to ten with an adorable dog, an entertaining sequence of spots gathered by the dog, and a surprise at the end. We have found that entertaining counting books like this help ensure an engaging and lively read-aloud experience with this kind of book!

Idea-enhancing books

Public libraries, school libraries, and classroom collections of children's books have many titles with great potential for exploring and discussing mathematics even though the plot or emphasis is not inherently mathematical. In our process of reading through and selecting books to read aloud, finding idea-enhancing books has felt like an exciting discovery: "This is such a great story! And if we include a focus on patterns or shapes or perspective, the story will be even *more* interesting!" These books do not have overt mathematical content like text-dependent books do. Instead, with a bit of thinking and noticing, we can find ways that mathematical ideas can enhance the story or make it more interesting. Some idea-enhancing books may be familiar to you and in your classroom collection already, while others may be new or less well known.

The Very Hungry Caterpillar (Carle 1969), a children's classic, is a well-known tale and an excellent example of an idea-enhancing book. Mathematics is not central to the story, nor is it part of the plot. Yet we wondered, what might children notice and wonder about the quantity of items the caterpillar ate on its weeklong eating adventure if they approached this story with a mathematical lens? Listening to children and looking at their representations as they kept track of what the caterpillar ate, we heard and saw that the caterpillar consumed many items—especially when it binged on Saturday! Turns out it ate twenty-five or twenty-six items depending on if you count the leaf, eaten on Sunday, as food. We listened to, and were inspired by, a lively debate about this among first-grade children who argued whether a leaf counts as food! Bringing mathematical ideas into this read-aloud enhanced children's experience with, and understanding of, the story.

Jabari Jumps (Cornwall 2017), the story we introduced in Chapters 1 and 2, is a delightful story about Jabari overcoming his fear of the high dive with some help and encouragement from his father. This story draws us in, and it is not overtly mathematical. But as an idea-enhancing book, we wondered about many mathematical questions such as, how high was the diving board? How far did Jabari jump before splashing into the water? How far did he submerge into the deep end of the pool? What is the relationship between the height of a diving board and the depth of a dive? Considering these questions helps us better understand the events in the story and how brave Jabari was as he conquered his fear. The illustrations add perspective to this consideration of distance; in one illustration, Jabari peers over the edge of the board to see the pool far, far below. Discussing distance and perspective in relation to Jabari's experiences adds meaning to the story—and this is the goal when selecting idea-enhancing books.

Illustration-exploring books

Many entertaining and lovely children's books are not mathematically focused and do not have any clear connection to mathematics. However, in our experience, most books have at least one mathematically interesting illustration that is worthy of exploration and discussion. These are illustration-exploring books, and they present exciting opportunities for a few moments of exploration during a read-aloud or when revisiting a page or two at another time.

The Snowy Day (Keats 1976) is a great example of an illustration-exploring book. This story is about a young boy who wakes up to see the snow and goes out exploring. He walks in the snow, pokes snow with a stick, makes snow angels, pretends to be a mountain climber, and packs a snowball to put in his pocket. The story doesn't feel, or jump out to readers, as mathematical. And yet . . . remember the illustration showing his sets of footprints in the snow? What happens if we pause, just for a moment during or after reading this story aloud, to notice these footprints and invite children to count them? "What do you notice about

the footprints? How many footprints do you see? How do you
see them?" In this illustration the boy is walking first with his
toes pointing out and then with his toes pointing in. If we pause
reading and look at this story with a mathematical lens, we see
sets of two footprints in a line and children readily begin counting by ones, twos, and a variety of combinations. Our exploration of this set of footprints is an example of using an
illustration-exploring book to invite children to notice

opportunities to count, to practice counting and sharing their counting strategies.

Hooray for Fish (Cousins 2017) is another good example of an illustration-exploring
book. It describes and shows a host of amazing and brilliantly colored unusual fish, including
one shaped like a pineapple and another resembling a strawberry! This book doesn't have a
mathematical plot. In fact, it has no plot at all. However, each illustration provides opportunities to think mathematically. For example, on one set of pages there is a large multi-
colored spotted fish upside down and a whole school of tiny
blue and white striped fish swirling in a circle around a small
orange fish. On these pages, we might pause and explore esti-
mation or counting or noticing playful patterns, asking, "How
many spots do you think there might be on the big upside-
down fish? How do you see these spots? How many little fish
do you think are swirling around the orange fish? How might
you count them? What patterns do you notice? How would
you describe your pattern?"

Wordless picture books also provide excellent opportunities for exploring illustrations. These books offer a series of
illustrations, often stunning and captivating visuals, that inspire
children to construct and narrate their own stories. For example, in the book *Flashlight* (Boyd 2014) illustrator Lizi Boyd
takes us along on a nighttime exploration in the woods.
Through charming and detailed black-and-white sketches,
children can notice and wonder—as mathematicians—about
exciting elements of nature that are revealed (and shown in
color) by the beam of the flashlight! A third-grade student,
Nasir, examining a page of *Flashlight* showing the beam of
light (Figure 3.2), noted: "I wonder about the way the flashlight is shining. It reminds me of a circle in fractions. Is it a
third or a fourth [of a circle] or more?"

Another student, Hala, wondered, "Why is the light shining so far, so long? If the owl held the flashlight more down [gesturing with her hand to show the flashlight at a steep angle toward the ground] the light would be more short. But [the flashlight] is more straight and so the light is shining long and we can see lots of animals!" Both Nasir and Hala noticed the light beam and made conjectures about the portion of light shining and how the angle of the flashlight affects the length of the light beam.

Figure 3.2
Flashlight Beam Illustration from the Book *Flashlight*

Illustration-exploring books provide rich opportunities, both planned and spontaneous, for noticing and discussing mathematics in the world around us. Once children become familiar with seeing stories with mathematical eyes, they excitedly examine all stories mathematically.

When we began studying books for mathematical potential, our question was, "Can any book be seen through a mathematical lens?" Over time, convinced that was true, our question became, "What happens when we view any story as a chance to think like mathematicians?"

Our big learnings around text types include:

- Consider all books as an opportunity to think mathematically.

- Notice that different books offer different mathematical opportunities.

- Be curious about how mathematics shows up in the story and illustrations.

- Depending on what students notice and wonder, a story may span text types.

Across all three book types, seeing stories through a mathematical lens brings curiosity and joy into read-aloud experiences and helps all children experience joy and wonder for mathematics. As you come to know the different text types and experiment with these ideas in your classroom, we hope you'll add on to our current understanding. We hope your innovations generate finer detail to our understanding of text types over time—that will be exciting!

Book Selection

You may be wondering, how do I select a book that is a good fit for the young mathematicians I am working with? A great hope for us is that students and teachers begin approaching *all* stories with a math lens. In this way, we hope that any story you're reading with students is an opportunity to think mathematically. And, we also understand that teachers carefully select the stories they read. When selecting a story to support young mathematicians, we have learned that there are different ways a teacher may go about choosing a book, depending on her purpose. One approach for book selection is finding a story that lends itself to further exploration of a mathematical idea currently being studied with students. The purpose of selecting a book in this case is to provide a fuller context in which children can think about a particular mathematical idea. Text-dependent books, which usually focus clearly on specific mathematical concepts, lend themselves to this approach. Another approach is to begin by selecting an engaging story and then inviting children to ask their own mathematical questions during the initial read-aloud. When using this approach, we are interested in supporting children to ask their own questions as mathematicians. All three book types work with this approach. The reasons we select a book varies, and each type of book offers different opportunities for exploring mathematical thinking through read-alouds and discussion. In Chapters 4 and 5 we explore three different approaches to read-alouds that work across text types and emphasize noticing and wondering, considering mathematical ideas and questions, and exploring story elements and events.

Selecting a Story to Think About Particular Mathematics

When we seek out stories that provide a context for thinking about a particular mathematical idea, we begin with certain mathematics in mind. For example, if children are learning about numbers and number combinations, we might choose a book like *Quack and Count* (Baker 1999). In this text-dependent story, a family of seven lively ducklings gets ready to fly for the first time, and young mathematicians can think within the story context and point to the illustrations as they reason about different numbers up to seven and ways to make seven. Each page and the accompanying illustration encourage the exploration of seven! As the story opens, it reads, "Seven ducklings in a row. Count those ducklings as they go!" The ducklings are lined up in a way that allows children to use the structure of the image to point and count by ones. We might choose to pause here and invite children to count aloud together as we point to each duckling, "Let's count these ducklings together: 1, 2, 3, 4, 5, 6, 7!" Recording those numbers on an easel as we count would allow us to note the symbolic representation, or we could trace the numbers in the air or just experience the joy of counting together!

On the next page of the story, one duckling separates from the brood, "Slipping, sliding, having fun. 7 ducklings, 6 plus 1." Here, the story context and the illustration support discussion about the idea that seven is made up on six and one more. We might pause to ask an open-ended question to surface these ideas, such as "What do you notice?" or a more targeted question, such as, "Where is the 6 plus 1 in this picture?" Again, we might record 6 + 1 = 7 or 7 = 6 + 1 on a chart paper to provide a visual representation of this number sentence (Figure 3.3). The story continues by opening up opportunities to think about numbers up to seven and the idea that numbers are made up of numbers. Children can see different groups of ducklings and prove that 7 = 5 + 2 or 7 = 4 + 3. They could also reason and argue about whether 7 = 6 + 1 is the same as 7 = 1 + 6 using the story context and the illustrations as an inspiration for their ideas.

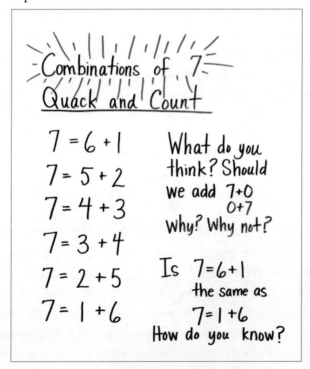

Figure 3.3
Combinations of Seven from *Quack and Count*

Quack and Count is an amusing story to explore together as readers, too, especially as children learn comprehension and language. The story lends itself to making predictions, as each page has the ducklings doing a different activity. This encourages children to predict what the ducklings might do on the next page and how many ducklings there may be. It also has an element of surprise, as at the end of the book all the ducklings take off, flying into the sky! Additionally, the text of the story is written utilizing rhyming pairs such as *row/go, fun/one, four/shore, dive/five*, and *six/tricks*, drawing attention to interesting words that sound the same but are spelled differently. We might write these rhyming pairs on chart paper so that children could begin noticing how these words sound and are written. Finally, the story contains a number of enticing action words that are shown in the illustrations: *slipping, sliding, splashing, paddling, flapping*, and *reaching* (Figure 3.4). We might try acting out these words in fun ways as a group, so that we could all experience the motions undertaken by the ducklings across the story!

Figure 3.4
Action Words from *Quack and Count*

Another example of selecting and reading a story to explore a particular mathematical concept can be found in *The Lion's Share* (McElligott 2012). In this text-dependent book, a group of animals is invited to dine with the lion. Each animal takes a portion of the cake, but the share they take, and their behavior, causes debate among readers about what is meant by *fair* and *equal* in this story about halving and doubling. To engage children in reasoning about portions, we might choose to read this story as a way of providing context for sensemaking discussion about fractions. Perhaps a group of children are beginning the formal study of fractions in school, or maybe a class is in the midst of studying fractions and questions are emerging about what portion a fraction represents. We explore read-alouds and discussions of *The Lion's Share* in upcoming chapters.

Stories selected based on particular mathematical ideas, like *Quack and Count* and *The Lion's Share*, tend to be text-dependent books. The mathematical ideas in text-dependent books are often easy to identify. *Quack and Count* supports thinking about combinations of seven. *The Lion's Share* supports thinking about halving and doubling. Since it is often easier to identify the mathematics within a text-dependent book, it can feel clear how to use a particular book to support thinking about a specific mathematical idea. We are constantly discovering stories that fall into this text-dependent category, and we are inspired by the ways a story context can be a powerful approach for seeding new mathematical ideas and for hearing and supporting children's current understandings and emerging mathematical ideas.

Along our journey in studying mathematizing, we have nudged ourselves to think beyond overtly mathematical books, to wonder about the mathematical potential in any story—idea-enhancing and illustration-exploring books. We can leverage the everyday activity of reading aloud and seeking out the mathematical opportunities in *any* story. So, what happens when we select a book that is not mathy? What happens when you begin from a more open stance?

Selecting an Engaging Story and Inviting Students to Think as Mathematicians and Readers

Rather than beginning with a mathematical concept and seeking out a story that can support sense making about that concept, it can be powerful to select a book simply because it is a beautiful or entertaining story and then to invite children to notice and wonder as mathematicians and readers. This open approach empowers children's mathematical agency and leads our classroom communities into interesting investigations.

The openness of inviting children to notice and wonder can feel scary at first. As teachers we may worry, will students notice anything? What if they notice things that are not the things I want them to notice? What if their noticings are not related to the math? These concerns are normal! Children always notice details and hearing their ideas is thrilling.

In the hilarious story *Stuck* (Jeffers 2011), Floyd's kite gets stuck in a tree. He surprises the reader by continuously throwing more and more items into the tree to try to get his kite unstuck! His shoe, his cat Mitch, a friend's bicycle, an orangutan, the house across the street, and even a whale end up in the tree! Floyd's emotions, gestures, and unpredictable ideas make for an entertaining read-aloud experience. While exploring this story, children noticed and wondered a variety of things (see the Noticings and Wonderings from *Stuck* chart).

Noticings and Wonderings from *Stuck*

- I notice the kite has pointy edges and angles—it gets especially stuck because of the points—it is like a diamond. If it was a circle, it might not get stuck in the tree.

- Floyd looks really mad when his shoe gets stuck. I can tell because his eyebrow is straight.

- I wonder if he's going to use the ladder to climb up into the tree and get the things out, and get them unstuck.

- I can't believe he threw the ladder into the tree!

- I notice the ladder is at an angle.

- I wonder what would happen if he threw things at different angles.

- I notice Floyd is really mad! Look at his arms and legs, he's jumping like when my sister has a fit.

- I notice the things he is throwing are getting bigger and bigger.

- Look at his legs and how he is balancing to hold the orangutan.

- I wonder if a rhinoceros is bigger than a barge?

- A tree could not hold that many things! There are 1, 2, 3, 4 . . . so many things. And most of them are enormous!

- I thought the firemen were going to get things out, not go in the tree, too.

- He's going to use the saw to cut down the tree! Nooooo, he threw the saw into the tree. You could throw a saw into a tree because some saws are not that heavy.

- I wonder if the tree could get full? Would something fall out?

In this open-ended read-aloud, mathematical ideas emerged (shape, angles, size, weight, volume, capacity) and literary ideas arose (irony, prediction, emotions). From students' ideas, we can reread the story (perhaps multiple times) and continue to delve into their thinking. For example, with students in the primary grades, we could highlight their noticing that

"A tree could not hold that many things!" and invite children to count aloud together as we point to the illustration. In doing so, we practice counting by ones or seeing items in groups, we hear students' current understanding of cardinality, and practice writing the symbolic notation for a number that represents the total. We have found there is power and potential in selecting books that are not tied to the ideas we are currently studying. This allows children to explore what they notice and wonder about and to steer our mathematical investigations.

Different books offer different mathematical opportunities. We find that the reasons for selecting a story can vary, depending on our purpose. We can strive to select stories that inspire discussion among children so that we can hear, understand, play with, and build upon their ideas. In upcoming chapters, we will explore interactive read-alouds from different perspectives—Open Notice and Wonder, Math Lens, and Story Explore. We use these different read-aloud approaches with all three text types described in this chapter.

Reflection and Discussion Questions

As you finish reading this chapter, here are some reflection questions for you to consider on your own or with colleagues:

1. As I glance at the books in my classroom library, what do I notice about the books I tend to read aloud? What read-aloud characteristics do the books in our classroom collection feature, and what characteristics might be absent? (See the box titled "Children's Literature Read-Aloud Characteristics" near the beginning of this chapter.)

2. What do I notice about the three text types in my collection? Do I tend to have text-dependent books, story-enhancing books, or illustration-exploring books, or a mix of all three types?

3. As I seek out and add new titles to my collections, which category will I bolster and why?

4. How am I identifying new books to create a classroom collection that represents all the children in our class and including books that are meaningful to and connect with their lives?

5. As I play with selecting books to mathematize with children, what opportunities do I notice when I select a story that supports thinking about a particular mathematical idea? What do I notice about enjoying an engaging story that does not match the mathematics we are currently working on? What are the opportunities and/or limitations of each approach?

Chapter 4

Open Notice and Wonder Reads

It's my job to engineer surprise. Students can only surprise us if we give them space and time and choice to surprise us.

—Tracy Zager, Math Coach

Look up from the pages of this book and glance at your surroundings. *What do you notice? What do you wonder?* As you give yourself a few moments to observe the details of your space, perhaps you will see something you have never noticed before! Now, take one more glimpse, narrowing upon details such as textures, patterns, colors, reflections, shapes, angles. *What do you notice? What do you wonder?* When we approach our world with these two questions, there is much to see, much to be curious about and ponder. There is always something to notice! There is always something of wonder! Noticing and wondering is a way of looking at our world.

We were inspired to notice and wonder from an amazing mathematician, Annie Fetter. Annie is an independent math educator, formerly from The Math Forum. She is an engaging speaker and writer who notices and wonders about mathematics everywhere in her world (e.g., when she is cooking, playing music, and exploring the outdoors). Annie has inspired our mathematics education community to engage in noticing and wondering on our own and with students.

Annie encourages us to ask *What do you notice?* and *What do you wonder?* to provide opportunities to hear children's thinking and communicate that children are sense makers who have valuable and useful mathematical ideas. Annie helps us to remember that children already are expert noticers and wonderers. As anyone who spends time with young children knows, they constantly share what they notice, and they always notice things we, as adults, don't "see" anymore. And how about those million "why?" questions children ask! We want to welcome children's noticings and wonderings and intentionally create openings for them to share their observations and curiosities. When we invite children to notice and wonder, every child has access to the discussion and every child can draw upon life experiences to observe and to ask questions. When we invite children to notice and wonder, their ideas and questions become central to our discussions; a culture of observation and curiosity is cultivated, and we communicate that mathematics is just as much about asking questions as it is about reasoning and problem solving. When we invite children to notice and wonder, we nurture the idea that mathematics is everywhere, and mathematicians are everywhere! Over time, and with repeated opportunities to practice, noticing and wondering become a habit of mind, and young mathematicians wear this lens as they approach their world.

We have taken up these questions, experimented with them alongside teachers and children, and learned there is great promise in beginning the exploration of a book with a first read that focuses on eliciting what children notice and wonder as they engage with a story. We have come to learn that beginning with an Open Notice and Wonder read-aloud is a time to enjoy a story as a classroom community. Sharing a book is a time to marvel; a time to understand the characters, setting, plot, and illustrations; to laugh, experience emotions, and fully get inside a story. It's also a time to listen for what children notice and wonder about mathematically, unprompted. It is a time to "engineer surprise" as Tracy Zager says. To allow children to surprise us with what they see and are curious about in the story. Together, we invest in the space and time necessary to appreciate stories and illustrations; to find joy for children's literature.

Getting Started: Open Notice and Wonder in First Grade

Perhaps the idea of sharing what you notice and wonder is already a routine in your classroom. Or maybe the idea of noticing and wondering is new to you and your students, especially when it comes to mathematizing children's literature. To hear what it sounds like to engage in an Open Notice and Wonder read-aloud experience, let's visit Ms. Hadreas and her first-grade students as they explore *Last Stop on Market Street* (de la Peña 2015). In this story, Nana and CJ ride the bus through San Francisco on their way to volunteer at a soup kitchen. This is an idea-enhancing book rich with opportunities to discuss and explore weighty themes and complex mathematics in ways that add to an understanding and appre-

ciation of the story. Ms. Hadreas selected this story (see the Read-Aloud Characteristics box in Chapter 3) because of the *visual interest* of its illustrations, the engaging *narrative pacing* of Nana and CJ's journey on the bus, the author's lyrical *literary style*, and the potential *emphasis* on ideas such as emotions and community. Mathematics is not central to the story or overt in the plot but has lots of potential to deepen students' understanding of story themes in many different ways. Ms. Hadreas and her first-grade students are engaging in their very first Open Notice and Wonder read-aloud and discussion as a new classroom community in the early autumn of a new school year.

| Ms. Hadreas: | Today we are going to explore the story *Last Stop on Market Street* written by Matt de la Peña and illustrated by Christian Robinson. As you look at the cover, I'm curious, what do you notice? What do you wonder? |

Mako: What does it mean to notice?

Ms. Hadreas: I'm so glad you asked that, Mako. Mako is asking, "What does it mean to notice?" When we notice, we observe, we pay attention to what we see. For example, when I look at this cover *(holding up the cover and pointing to the illustration)*, I notice, or I see, a child holding hands with a person. What do you notice? What do you see? Turn and tell your neighbor.

With the book cover displayed under the document camera, Ms. Hadreas kneels down next to children to listen to their noticings. She jots herself a few notes to record what she hears. She wants to revoice students' ideas to support the norm that we listen to each other well enough to repeat what others say. She also wants to communicate to students that their ideas are heard and valued and at the heart of their classroom discussions.

Ms. Hadreas: *(Bringing the children back together)* Wow, I can hear that you are noticing many things on the cover of this book. I hear Julyssa and Olivia noticing the bus, Dylan and Satchel saw the bus stop sign, and Avery, you pointed out the round wheel. I hear students noticing the rider with the green scarf with white polka dots and the rider with the orange hat. Some of you noticed the bus driver sitting up front. As you look at the cover, I'd also like you to think about what you wonder. When we wonder, we are curious, and we ask questions. What questions do you have? What do you wonder? Turn and tell your neighbor.

Again, Ms. Hadreas kneels beside children to listen to their ideas so she can repeat what they wonder. She is careful to note the ideas of children who she had not yet repeated in the whole group so she could position all students as competent in this community.

Ms. Hadreas: You are curious about so many things! Lulu, I hear you wondering about the child. Some of you, like Frankie and Millie, said you wonder if the child is a boy with his mom or grandma. I hear others wondering where the bus is going. And where the bus came from. Let's read and find out!

Opening the pages of the book, Ms. Hadreas reads the title page and begins reading the story, holding up the book for children to follow along. Small sticky notes mark the pages where she anticipates pausing to invite children to share what they are noticing and wondering (see Figure 4.1). She will follow students' interests and either stick with her planned stopping spots (marked by the sticky notes) or adjust her plan to honor what she is hearing children say.

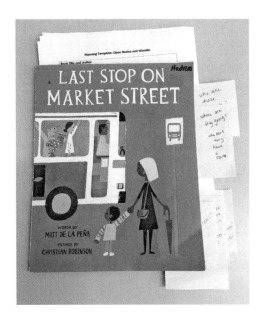

Figure 4.1
Ms. Hadreas's Anticipated Stopping Points for *Last Stop on Market Street*

Before we venture into the story and discussion with Ms. Hadreas and her students, let's pause to notice some of the decisions she made as she introduced the story. In this introduction of an Open Notice and Wonder read-aloud, Mako asked what it meant to notice. Ms. Hadreas had anticipated that her students might ask for help in knowing what the words *notice* and *wonder* mean, especially since this is a new routine in her classroom. She thought ahead of time about how to describe those words, if children asked, and had sketched some ideas on her planning sheet. She decided she would describe noticing as what we *see* or what we *observe*. She would describe wondering as what we are *curious* about or what *questions* we have. She offered her students some sentence starters as options to support their language (Figure 4.2). She hoped these sentence starters would support students to know what it can sound like to share their noticings and wonderings. She also valued their natural ways of phrasing their ideas and made them available as inspiration as children used their own words. If noticing and wondering is new in your classroom community, you may want to develop working definitions of these words with your students, also. Although these may be new words to students, children are natural at noticing and wondering, and it will not take long for these questions to take hold and become a regular part of the way you communicate all throughout the school day!

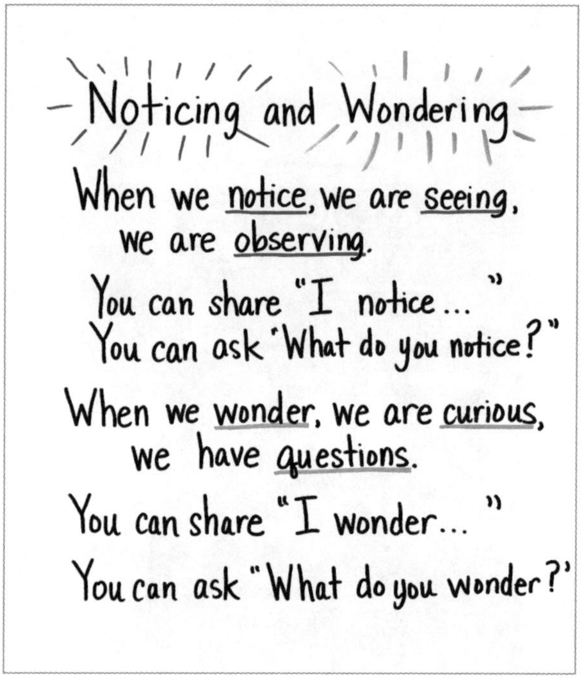

Figure 4.2
Noticing and Wondering Chart

A few pages in, the characters CJ and his Nana (the child and adult visible on the cover) are waiting at the bus stop. CJ waves to his friend who is driving away in a car with his dad. CJ asks, "Nana, how come we don't got a car?" Ms. Hadreas had flagged this as an anticipated stopping point to invite children to share what they were noticing and wondering so far in the story.

Ms. Hadreas: Let's pause here. What do you notice? What do you wonder?

During the first read of this story, Ms. Hadreas's plan is to ask two questions—
What do you notice? and *What do you wonder?*—every time she pauses. Since
her goal is to help children get inside the story context, she will continue to invite
them to notice and to wonder even though it can be tempting to ask other
questions! She hears:

> "I notice some people have umbrellas."

> "I notice puddles. I see rain."

> "I wonder why it smelled like freedom."

> "I wonder why she said the tree drinks through a straw."

> "I notice the boy said, 'How come we don't have a car?' I wonder
> why they don't have a car."

> "My family doesn't have a car. We ride the bus!"

As children share their ideas aloud, Ms. Hadreas captures their thinking on chart
paper. She uses a blue marker to capture noticings and green marker to capture
wonderings. After recording students' ideas, Ms. Hadreas continues reading.
While she reads, she senses that students have *a lot* to say about the next few
pages, so she adapts her plan in the moment and creates an additional pause to
let the students share their noticings and wonderings, including:

> "I notice there is a dragon that breathes fire on the side of the
> bus!"

> "I notice the bus is number 5 and it is going to Market Street."

> "That is the name of the book!"

> "No, I think the bus is number 0923, see!" *(Pointing to the
> numbers on the front of the bus beneath the driver's window)*

"I wonder how the bus driver pulled that coin out from behind CJ's ear."

"Did he let CJ keep that coin?"

"I wonder how the old woman catches the butterflies in the jar."

"I notice CJ's grandma is knitting a scarf."

"I think she is knitting a purse!"

"Nana's earrings are green triangles."

"That man has tattoos."

"The lady in the striped shirt is facing that way and all the other people are facing this way."

"Nana hangs her umbrella on the railing."

"Why is there a dog on the bus?"

"The dog has a blue coat."

"I think it is because some people use dogs to help them walk. And, he has a cane."

"I notice he looks calm when his eyes are closed like the dogs."

Ms. Hadreas: Wow! I'm so glad you are sharing what you think! What you notice. What you wonder. You are paying such close attention to the details in the story and in the illustrations. That is exciting!

Ms. Hadreas is glad she revised her plan for the next anticipated stopping point and created time for students to share their observations and thoughts. By adding in another stopping point, she can hear that they were getting inside the story details. She is often joyfully surprised by the details children notice—Nana's green triangle earrings, the dog wearing the blue coat—and welcomes all ideas in an Open Notice and Wonder discussion. The goal of the discussion is to get inside the story—not a reading strategy or a math skill—and to enjoy experiencing the story together. Even when children share a tiny detail or if what they share isn't about math, she creates time to listen to the details that students notice. Children's ideas help her think about where they may go next in future reads of this story. She continues reading and then stops where she had planned, when CJ is listening to the music.

Ms. Hadreas: What do you notice? What do you wonder?

"I see butterflies and birds."

"I notice the moon."

"He has on his same sweater."

"I notice CJ is closing his eyes and feeling the magic!"

"I wonder if he is really seeing sunsets and waves?"

"I notice he's feeling magic inside of him."

Ms. Hadreas: He's feeling the magic! Let's all close our eyes like CJ. Let's spread our arms open wide. Let's imagine we're listening to the guitar man play. Can you hear the music? Can you feel the magic?

Reading on, she pauses at her last two anticipated, and planned for, stopping points. Next, as CJ and Nana got off the bus, students notice that bus riders were clapping, CJ put his coin from the bus driver into the guitar man's hat, and Nana waved goodbye to the driver. They wonder if CJ is happy because he looked like he was smiling and jumping off the bus. Finally, she stops at the illustration of the soup kitchen. Students notice many of the same people they saw on earlier pages, such as the woman with the red hat. They notice that CJ is still smiling and that he is holding a bowl and passing it to Nana. They wonder why CJ and

Nana are serving soup, why there are so many people there, and what kind of soup they are eating. With the students' noticings and wonderings captured (see Figure 4.3), they wrap up the discussion. Ms. Hadreas is eager to step back and look at the ideas and think about where to go next with this story.

Open |Notice| and |Wonder|:
    Last Stop on Market Street

Some people have umbrellas
puddles and rain
Why does it smell like freedom
Why the tree drinks through a straw
CJ said "How come we don't have a car?"
Why don't they have a car
a fire breathing dragon on the side of the bus
bus is 5. going to Market Street
bus is 0923
how did bus driver pull coin from CJ's ear
how did woman catch butterflies in jar?
Nana is knitting a scarf or a purse
Her earrings are green triangles
The man has tattoos
Some people are facing different directions
Nana's umbrella is on the railing
Why is there a dog on the bus?!
Dog has a blue coat
CJ looks calm when his eyes are closed (like the dog)
Butterflies, birds, the moon, his same sweater
CJ closes his eyes and feels the magic
is he really seeing sunsets and waves?
He is feeling magic inside

Figure 4.3
Ms. Hadreas's Class Chart from Open Notice and Wonder Read of *Last Stop on Market Street*

Planning for an Open Notice and Wonder in Your Classroom

Planning for an Open Notice and Wonder read-aloud is a straightforward four-step process:

1. Read the story to yourself and engage in your own notice and wonder.

2. Anticipate what your students might notice and wonder.

3. Plan for the story launch by looking at the cover of the book and thinking about how to introduce it.

4. Prepare for the read-aloud itself by posting a few blank pieces of chart paper and collecting a couple of different-colored markers to prepare for charting children's ideas.

Once you have selected a work of children's literature based on the read-aloud characteristics in Chapter 3 (and perhaps ideas from Chapter 2 about book selection), the *first step* in planning an Open Notice and Wonder read-aloud is to read the story to yourself and engage in your own notice and wonder. Before reading with children, enjoy the story and ask yourself, *What do I notice? What do I wonder?* An important element of this first read is that you enjoy the story! Give yourself permission to take a few moments of your day to find delight within a story and its illustrations. Knowing the story context and the details of the illustrations helps us think about what is possible within that story in deeper, more thoughtful way.

Let's try noticing and wondering together! Here is a page from *City Shapes* written by Diana Murray and illustrated by Bryan Collier (Figure 4.4). As you look at this illustration, what do you notice? What do you wonder? Take your time. What do you see? Keep looking!

Figure 4.4
Two-Page Spread in *City Shapes*

When we (Tony and Allison) look at this illustration, we have similar noticings and some excitingly different wonderings. Tony notices circles all over the pages, like bubbles floating around. He notices the girl peering into a kaleidoscope. He wonders, what does she see? He notices she has a star on her shirt. He notices the balloons. He wonders what occasion the balloons are there to help celebrate. Is it a birthday? An anniversary? Maybe a baby shower or graduation? Tony notices a girl drawing with chalk on the pavement. He wonders, what is she drawing? What is she thinking about as she draws? Where is her mom or dad or the rest of her family? Are they the people with the balloons? He notices the pigeon again. He's seen it before in the story. He wonders what the pigeon signifies and where it is going. Tony notices a flower bed. He wonders if they are begonias. He wonders if they get enough water or too much sun. He wonders who designed the park. He notices that it looks architecturally interesting in terms of landscaping, with grassy areas and flower beds, short retaining walls and mature trees. He notices the red umbrellas in the background. He wonders if there are refreshments nearby, if there is a hot dog stand, and what kinds of snacks and treats people can buy near this park.

When Allison looks at this page, she also notices the girl in the star shirt who is looking through the kaleidoscope. She notices pieces of colorful glass have settled in the bottom of the circle on the front. She notices both of the girl's hands holding the viewing tube. Allison wonders if she is rotating the sections and what reflections or patterns are bringing a smile to the girl's face. Is there symmetry in the patterns? She notices circles. She wonders if they are iridescent bubbles because the circles by the trees and over the flowers and plants seem to be brown, pink, or green. She notices the colorful balloons. There is a group of five balloons behind the tree and one more pink balloon in front of the tree, on the handlebars of a child's scooter. Allison notices the pigeon that is so fun to follow through this story. She wonders if the pigeon has landed to nibble a seed or berry that was dropped on the park path or maybe to appreciate the chalk rainbow. She notices the chalk artist, and she notices that both girls are wearing patterned headbands. She notices people in the distance and red umbrellas. Some details of this illustration look like photographs. She wonders how the illustrator incorporated photographs with drawings. She wonders if the girl with the kaleidoscope is someone that the illustrator knows.

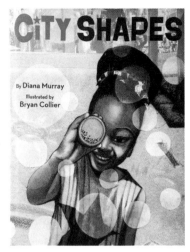

We find noticing and wondering to be a joyful experience. We each come to a story and illustrations with our own perspective, ideas, and life experiences that shape what we see and what we find curious. As teachers, we want to create space for ourselves to notice details and to be curious as readers and mathematicians. Just as we honor the lenses children bring to our classrooms, we can honor, nurture, and expand our own lenses.

The *second step* in planning an Open Notice and Wonder read-aloud, after you've read the story yourself, is to anticipate what your students might notice and wonder. Knowing your students well, what do you think they might they see and hear in this story that is interesting or curious to them? As you anticipate your students' experience with the story, you can also anticipate where you might pause while reading to invite students to share what they are noticing and wondering. Place a sticky note on those pages to remind yourself of your plan. Since children's books do not tend to have page numbers, in addition to the sticky note, we often jot a feature of the page on the planning sheet (such as a quote or something significant in the illustration).

We tend to aim for identifying a few (three to five) key stopping points where there is an opportunity for sense making. For example, maybe you anticipate pausing at a place in the story that is ripe for making a prediction (there may be an unknown element of surprise on the next page), or maybe you want to pause when a character is experiencing a big emotion that is an opportunity for students to practice empathy, or maybe something interesting mathematically is happening in the story or in a particular illustration that might provide opportunities for pausing to notice and wonder. We strive to seldom pause, in intentional instances, so we keep the momentum of the read and joy for the story, while also creating ample space to hear children's ideas. There are many reasons why you may anticipate pausing to discuss the story, and as teachers we're always ready to revise our plan, depending on students' energy and what they are curious about exploring (just as Ms. Hadreas did when her students had a lot to say about pages she didn't anticipate pausing on). Being attuned to students' curiosity often requires that we make on-the-spot decisions about when to revise our plans and why.

The *third step* is to plan for the story launch by looking at the cover of the book and thinking about how to introduce it. What is shown on the cover that would help pique children's interest and get them excited to explore the story? What might you model by thinking aloud to demonstrate what it means to notice and to wonder about something in the cover illustration? You'll notice that the planning sheet invites you to anticipate stopping points and then move on to planning a launch. This is because planning for stopping points (which involves reading and thinking about the story ourselves) informs planning of the launch. In this way, the planning process happens in a slightly different order than facilitation plays out.

The *fourth step* is to prepare for the read-aloud itself by posting a few blank pieces of chart paper and collecting a couple of different-colored markers to prepare for charting children's ideas. The questions you ask during the read will remain the same: *What do you notice? What do you wonder?* As children share what they notice and wonder, chart their ideas. We try using different colors to record their noticings and wonderings. This allows us to go back as a group and see where we noticed details and where we wondered and had thoughts and questions as readers and mathematicians.

Charting Ideas

There are many reasons we think charting students' ideas is important. When we take the time to hear and record students' thinking, it helps them see their ideas are important. It helps us make sure we are understanding their thinking. It gives us a common artifact to think about each other's ideas. It provides a written record for future discussions and explorations of the story. Charted ideas help students see we are thinking carefully about their ideas and use their thinking to make decisions about where to go next or what to explore in upcoming read-alouds.

As we have played with charting ideas that emerge in an Open Notice and Wonder read-aloud, we recognize that this is not easy! We try to listen, to keep up with the ideas and capture what we hear, and to toggle between marker colors. As you give an Open Notice and Wonder read a try, we encourage you to be playful and see what works best for you and your students. Sometimes we stop fewer times to notice and wonder, allowing us more time to chart students' ideas. Other times we have students turn and talk to a think partner about what they are noticing and wondering, asking just a few volunteers to share their ideas so we can chart them and move on more quickly. Additionally, we have on occasion jotted down student noticings and wonderings on a clipboard, transferring these ideas to chart paper later to be ready for the next read-aloud and discussion.

As we launch a subsequent read, we tend to refer back to the chart to tell students what we plan to think more about in this next read. We also tend to circle ideas that become the focus of subsequent read-alouds so that students see the continuity in sequence. We can keep an eye for what students are noticing and wondering and thinking about, and we anchor our read-aloud plans and enactments in these ideas.

Open Notice and Wonder Planning Template

We have put together the steps for planning an Open Notice and Wonder read-aloud into a planning template that we use to sketch our ideas before exploring the book we've selected with students (Figure 4.5). A blank version of the Open Notice and Wonder planning template can be found in Appendix A.

As an example, see the ideas Ms. Hadreas sketched in her planning template in Figure 4.6. The writing in the planning template conveys her ideas— what she notices, what she wonders, what she plans to say during the read-aloud. Jotting down her ideas on the template helps Ms. Hadreas keep her thoughts about the book in mind while also carefully listening to and charting her students' noticings and wonderings.

OPEN NOTICE AND WONDER

Book Title and Author

○ **Read and enjoy the story.**
As teacher and reader, what do I notice? What do I wonder?

○ **Anticipate and mark intended places for pausing the story.**
What do I anticipate will be interesting or curious to my students? Where do I anticipate pausing to invite students to share? Why? Place sticky note on the pages.

○ **Plan for story launch.**
With my stopping points in mind, how will I introduce the story using the cover? What might students notice and wonder on the cover?

○ **Gather chart paper and different-colored markers.**

Figure 4.5
Planning Template for Open Notice and Wonder

OPEN NOTICE AND WONDER

Book Title and Author: <u>Last Stop on Market Street</u> by Matt de la Peña

Read and enjoy the story.
As teacher and reader, what do I notice? What do I wonder?

I notice CJ's questions ("how come . . . ?").

I notice Nana's perspective ("always found beautiful") and Nana and CJ's relationship.

I notice the community of people on the bus and in the soup kitchen.

I wonder—Where are CJ and Nana going on the bus? What will they do once they get there?

Anticipate and mark intended places for pausing the story.
What do I anticipate will be interesting or curious to my students?
Where do I anticipate pausing to invite students to share? Why?

Place sticky note on the pages.

Anticipate pausing points on these pages—

1. When CJ and Nana are waiting at the bus stop ("how come we don't got a car?")
2. When CJ and Nana are on the bus (guitar player and "feel the magic of music")
3. When CJ and Nana are getting off the bus
4. When CJ and Nana are in the soup kitchen

Plan for story launch.
With my stopping points in mind, how will I introduce the story using the cover? What might students notice and wonder on the cover?

- "Let's take a look at the cover of our book, Last Stop on Market Street. I'm so curious about what you notice and wonder about this cover."
- "When we notice, we share what we observe or see."
- "When we wonder, we share what we are curious about or what questions we have."
- On the cover, I anticipate students may notice the bus, the passengers on the bus, the bus driver, the bus stop, a child and adult, shapes (such as rectangles and circles), the pattern on the child's sleeves.
- On the cover, I anticipate students may wonder about the characters and where they are going on the bus.

Gather chart paper and different-colored markers.
Place chart paper and markers within reach for charting students' ideas.

Figure 4.6
Ms. Hadreas's Planning Template for Open Notice and Wonder About *Last Stop on Market Street*

Open Notice and Wonder in Third Grade

As her third-grade students gather on the carpet, Ms. Burris prepares the easel with chart paper and selects a few different-colored markers. She sits down beside her students, holding a copy of *The Lion's Share* (McElligott 2012), a text-dependent book focused on the concepts of halving and doubling, in her lap. On this spring afternoon, she plans to read the first half of the story, which focuses on the mathematical idea of halving. Engaging in Open Notice and Wonder read-alouds has become a routine in this classroom community, and today she is excited to hear students' thinking within this mathematical tale of Lion's dinner party. As the guests cut the cake, each taking one half of the remaining cake, the animals' ideas of what is equal evoke response, and often outrage, from her students! Ms. Burris selected this book (referring to the read-aloud characteristics in Chapter 3) for its emphasis on the ideas of *half*, *equal*, and *fair*, for its *visual interest*, and for what she anticipated would be engaging and animated student experiences in response to the story's theme of fairness and the unjust treatment of others. Ms. Burris is excited to hear what her students will come up with in this Open Notice and Wonder read and specifically what they might notice or wonder about mathematically. During today's Open Notice and Wonder read-aloud, she plans to read the first half of the book (the portion on halving). Figure 4.7 shows Ms. Burris's thoughts about facilitating this Open Notice and Wonder read. In a future read, they will continue into the second half of the book (which is focused on doubling).

OPEN NOTICE AND WONDER

Book Title and Author: The Lion's Share by Matthew McElligott

Read and enjoy the story.
As teacher and reader, what do I notice? What do I wonder?
I notice Ant and Lion are well mannered (Ant on time, Lion generous and patient).
I notice other animals are not well mannered (late, rude, bad table manners).
I notice each animal took half, which doesn't seem fair.
I notice Ant's piece was too small to divide.
I wonder why Lion invited such awful dinner guests?
I wonder what will Ant do, and how will the other animals respond?

OPEN NOTICE AND WONDER (continued)

Anticipate and mark intended places for pausing the story.
What do I anticipate will be interesting or curious to my students?
Where do I anticipate pausing to invite students to share? Why?

Place sticky note on the pages.
My anticipated pausing points—
  1. At the dinner party (strange manners)
  2. When the cake divided (each animal cuts cake in half)
  3. Ant's generous offer
Planning to read the first half of the story today (reading through the portion of halving, stopping before the portion on doubling).

Plan for story launch.
With my stopping points in mind, how will I introduce the story using the cover?
What might students notice and wonder on the cover?

"Let's take a look at the cover of our book, The Lion's Share. I'm so curious about what you notice and wonder about this cover."
I anticipate students may notice Lion, Ant, crumbs on the table, and the play on words with "halving" for "having."
I anticipate students may wonder about who the characters are and what they are going to do.

Gather chart paper and different-colored markers.
Place chart paper and markers within reach for charting students' ideas.

Figure 4.7
Ms. Burris's Sketched-in Planning Template for
Open Notice and Wonder Read-Aloud of *The Lion's Share*

Ms. Burris: As we read this story (*holding up* The Lion's Share), I will pause, as we tend to do together, to invite you to share what you are noticing and what you are wondering. This book is called *The Lion's Share: A Tale of Halving Cake and Eating It, Too.* As you look at the cover, what do you think this story will be about and what makes you think that? Turn and talk with your neighbor about your ideas.

As Ms. Burris listens in on students sharing their ideas, she charts their noticings and wonderings. She continues charting students' ideas across the Open Notice and Wonder read (see Figure 4.8).

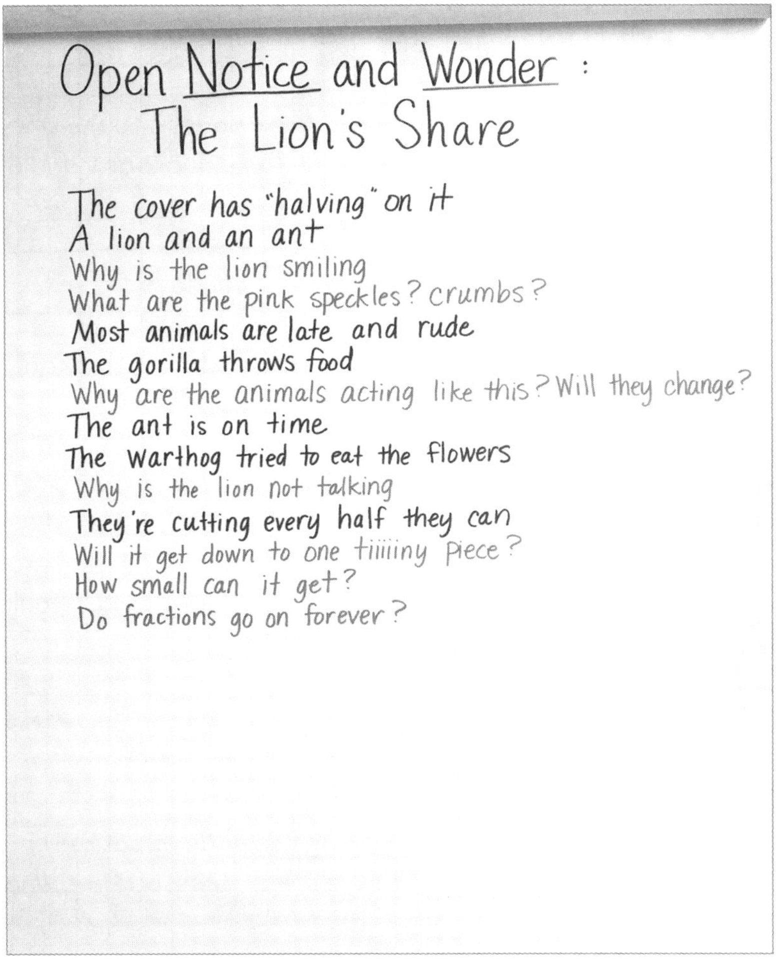

Open <u>Notice</u> and <u>Wonder</u> :
The Lion's Share

The cover has "halving" on it
A lion and an ant
Why is the lion smiling
What are the pink speckles? crumbs?
Most animals are late and rude
The gorilla throws food
Why are the animals acting like this? Will they change?
The ant is on time
The warthog tried to eat the flowers
Why is the lion not talking
They're cutting every half they can
Will it get down to one tiiiiiny piece?
How small can it get?
Do fractions go on forever?

Figure 4.8
Charted Ideas from Ms. Burris's Class Open Notice and Wonder Read-Aloud of *The Lion's Share*

Adisa: I notice that the cover has the word *halving* on it.

Kazuo: I notice an ant and a lion.

Aram: I wonder why it looks like the lion is smiling.

Grace:	I wonder what those pink speckles are—they look like crumbs and maybe since it says cake, they are cake crumbs.
Ms. Burris:	*(As she finishes charting students' ideas)* You noticed and wondered about so many interesting things. Let's dive into the book and find out more!

Ms. Burris opens the book and begins reading. A few pages into the story, after the animals have been invited to, and arrived at, the dinner party and dinner has been served, she pauses.

Ms. Burris:	What do you notice? What do you wonder?
Leo:	I notice most of the animals were late to the party and they made really bad choices at dinner!
Ms. Burris:	How might you use the illustrations to show your thinking?
Leo:	They're making a mess and throwing food. Like here *(pointing to the illustration)* where Gorilla throws his food. I would be in big trouble if I threw food at a party!
Abby:	I wonder why the animals are acting like this and if they will change?
Ms. Burris:	Yes, there is much to notice on this page about the characters at the party! Turn and talk with your think partner, what do you notice? What do you wonder?

Listening in, Ms. Burris can hear students in animated conversations about the animals at the party. There is a hint of amusement among these nine- and ten-year-old students as well as a twinge of surprise and horror! She wants to nurture these noticings because analyzing the characters' behaviors will likely lead to more spirited dialogue about what is fair and just in subsequent reads and discussions.

Ms. Burris: Let's come back together! I can hear you have *big* ideas about what is happening at this dinner party so far. Let's hear a few more noticings and wonderings.

Roshann: I notice the ant is on time and doesn't want animals to throw food.

Neeku: We noticed that the warthog tried to eat the flowers!

Elliot: I wonder why the lion is not talking.

Ms. Burris: Let's read on and see what happens next! What do you think will happen next, and how do you know?

As the story continues, a cake is brought out for dessert. Elephant makes the first cut of the cake, taking half for himself. One by one, each animal cuts half of the remaining cake and passes on the rest for the next animal. Once the pattern of cutting in half is established, Ms. Burris chooses to pause and discuss what students are noticing and wondering and what they are predicting will happen next.

Johan: I notice they're cutting every half they can. I predict the lion will not get any cake.

Naomi: I wonder if it will get down to one tiiiiiiny little piece? *(Holding her hand up to show a smidgen of space between her fingers)* I think it will get too small.

Jasper: I wonder how small it can get and if fractions go on forever?

Beyond Notice and Wonder: Questions as Refrain

The Open Notice and Wonder approach reminds us of Maria Nichols's emphasis, in her book *Comprehension Through Conversation*, on the importance of asking open-ended questions in reading and discussing books to support children's thinking and understanding. She writes,

> When planning our questions, we need to start with open-ended questions that offer the children an opportunity to think strategically, share their thinking, and do the work for themselves before supporting the effort with more specific questions. Often, we give children too much information, embedding what we hope to hear in the question. (2006, 56)

Having a few open-ended questions we can rely on to ask at any time, in any read-aloud, is helpful. For example, as teachers we often ask children, *Can you tell me more about your thinking?* or *How do you know that?* in addition to *What do you notice?* and *What do you wonder?* We have a short list of questions like these that we carry with us during any read-aloud experience, whether it's an Open Notice and Wonder read-aloud or a more focused one. We call these "questions as refrain," and we find they work well with almost any text to hear children's thinking and nurture their exploration of ideas (Figure 4.9).

Questions such as "How might you use the illustrations to show your thinking?" that Ms. Burris asked Leo, or "What will happen next? How do you know?" that Johan, Naomi, and Jasper responded to (in the previous vignette) allow us to hear more about, and more deeply understand, children's thinking. These questions can be used in a wide range of contexts and are universally friendly for opening up discussion. When we think about what to ask next, we want our questions to be genuine and in response to what we are hearing children say, *and* it can sometimes be challenging to think of what to ask to encourage children's thinking and sense making about complex mathematics. We have found that these open-ended questions as refrain help students explore multiple story dimensions as readers and mathematicians and to generate noticings and wonderings about the story. For example, nearly every children's story has illustrations, and when we ask children, "How might you use the illustrations to show your thinking?" the images become a tool to help

GUIDING QUESTIONS
Questions as Refrain

MATH
- What do you see, notice, or wonder about?
- What (numbers, combinations, patterns, shapes, other math concept) do you see?
- How might you use the illustrations to show your thinking?

LITERACY
- What do you think will happen in this story, and why do you think so?
- What will happen next? How do you know?
- What connections can you make between this story and another story or something else you know?

Figure 4.9
Questions as Refrain
Foldable Bookmark

children think and to explain their thinking. Perhaps a child will point to the illustration and use one-to-one correspondence to count all of the items. Or perhaps items are clustered in small groups on a page, and a child sees a group of three and then counts on. Having a visual to point to can help children develop their ideas, explain their thinking, and help us understand their thinking.

The questions we ask over and over again become a part of who we are as a community. Children internalize our community's questions and are more likely to ask them of themselves and each other in our conversations. We invite you to print out the questions as refrain bookmark (Appendix B) and tuck it in your pocket or carry it with you through the pages of a book to inspire how you respond to children's ideas within the story. We invite you to expand on these questions, making them your own in your community.

There is great value in reading the same story multiple times with children. Beginning with a first read-aloud that aims to enjoy the story, and come to know the story context, allows us to get inside and think about the context in meaningful ways. A powerful way to immerse in a story context is to invite children to notice and wonder. Using the prompts of *What do you notice?* and *What do you wonder?* we can support children to observe and be curious, and we can hear their ideas and use those ideas to inspire further discussions. We can also practice, as teachers, asking open-ended questions where there are infinite answers and all children are empowered to explore ideas through discussion and problem solving.

Reflection and Discussion Questions

As you finish reading this chapter, here are some reflection questions for you to consider on your own or with colleagues:

1. In my upcoming lessons, where do I see opportunities for an Open Notice and Wonder read-aloud? Which stories might we read and why?

2. How do I want to introduce noticing and wondering to my students? Or deepen our practices around noticing and wondering as a classroom community?

3. Which open-ended questions do I tend to pose to students? Which questions as refrain would I like to try and why?

4. What am I noticing about how a story context offers different opportunities than a story problem? What more would I like to explore with this idea?

Chapter 5
Focused Reads:
Story Explore and Math Lens

My question is not always the question
students want to think about.
–Kassia Wedekind, Math Coach

Stepping back from the ideas she charted during the Open Notice and Wonder read-aloud of *Last Stop on Market Street* (de la Peña 2015), Ms. Hadreas thinks about what her first-grade students shared the previous day. Her students noticed and wondered so many things she didn't anticipate or see herself (see Figure 4.3). Students noticed that Nana is knitting a scarf, CJ closes his eyes and feels the magic, and the bus stopping on Market Street matches the book title. Students wondered why it smelled like freedom, why CJ and Nana don't have a car, how the lady on the bus caught the butterflies, and why there was a dog on the bus.

Ms. Hadreas thinks about her students' ideas and considers where to go in the next discussions about this story and why. She decides to focus the next read on literary elements of the story, such as CJ's character and how his feelings change as the story progresses, knowing this would connect both to students' lives and to deeper themes of community, belongingness, and poverty. Ms. Hadreas also decides that after the literary-focused read, a math-focused read could come last, giving her and her students an opportunity to explore Nana and CJ's community in a quantitative way to add depth to students' understanding of community.

When planning for and facilitating subsequent read-alouds and discussions, our aim is to take up ideas that students generate in the Open Notice and Wonder read-aloud and explore them more deeply, delving into the mathematical and literary ideas in meaningful ways. Sometimes our goal is to focus on the literary noticings and wonderings of the story and further explore the plot, characters, vocabulary, or themes. We call this a *Story Explore* read. Other times, our goal is to think more about the mathematical noticings and wonderings and revisit the story as mathematicians. We call this a *Math Lens* read. These two discussion structures are *focused*, zooming in on literacy or mathematics, as compared with the openness of an Open Notice and Wonder read. To better understand these two read-aloud discussion structures and the connections between them, let's drop in again on Ms. Hadreas and her first-grade students as they reread *Last Stop on Market Street* and Ms. Burris and her intermediate students as they reread *The Lion's Share* (McElligott 2012).

Story Explore in a Primary-Grade Classroom:
Last Stop on Market Street

As Ms. Hadreas reviews her students' charted ideas, she is drawn to a particular noticing, "I notice he [CJ] closes his eyes and feels the magic." When Mako shared this noticing, he acted out the "feeling the magic" just as it showed CJ in the illustration (Figure 5.1).

And in the darkness,
the rhythm lifted CJ out of the bus,
out of the busy city.

He saw sunset colors swirling over crashing waves.
Saw a family of hawks slicing through the sky.
Saw the old woman's butterflies
dancing free in the light of the moon.
CJ's chest grew full and he was lost in the sound
and the sound gave him the feeling of magic.

Figure 5.1
CJ Feeling the Magic Illustration from *Last Stop on Market Street*

Ms. Hadreas decides to pursue this noticing. She wants her students to pay attention to and understand how CJ's feelings change across the story. This change in character feelings becomes the focus of her Story Explore read. She hopes this exploration will support students in having thoughtful conversations about CJ's experiences and his relationship with Nana, as well as help students make meaningful connections to their own feelings. She sketches in a planning template (Figure 5.2). For a blank copy of the Planning Template for a Focused Read, see Appendix C.

FOCUSED READ

Book Title and Author: Last Stop on Market Street written by Matt de la Peña, illustrated by Christian Robinson

Discussion Structure
◉ Story Explore
○ Math Lens

Order of Read
◉ 2nd read
○ 3rd read
○ Other

Making Connections
Which ideas from the first Open Notice and Wonder read (and/or the Story Explore or Math Lens read) do I want to pursue? Why?

> There are lots of times in this book where CJ feels something. Point out Open Notice and Wonder ideas:

> "I notice that he is . . . closing his eyes and feeling the magic."

What portion of the story will I reread?

◉ Entire story
○ Part of the story
○ Revisit illustration(s)

Where Might We Pause and Why?

Page (Description)	Story Explore or Math Lens Question/Prompt
P. 5 (Church doors)	How might CJ be feeling as he skips down the steps?
P. 8 (How come we don't got a car)	How is CJ feeling right now, when he asks, "How come we don't got a car?"
P. 12 (Having just boarded the bus)	How might CJ be feeling when the driver does that magic trick for him? Do you think they know people on this bus, and why do you think that?
P. 14 (Four people on bus, sitting in a row)	How is he feeling now, and why do you think that?
P. 18 (Guitar player already plucking strings)	How is CJ feeling? He doesn't have a music player. What do you think? Is there ever a time you wanted something but weren't able to get it? Whisper to a neighbor, say, "One time . . ."
P. 20 (Feeling the magic)	Is he still feeling sad? How might you describe his feelings on this page?
P. 22 (Getting off bus—Last Stop on Market Street)	What do you notice? How is CJ feeling now?
P. 28 (In line to enter soup kitchen)	Has he been here before? Is this a place he goes? How is CJ feeling now, and how do you know?
P. 30 (Helping serve in the soup kitchen)	What are CJ and Nana doing? How do you think he's feeling being there? How do you know?

How Will I Launch the Story?

Reread the page where CJ feels the magic. Mention his feelings and that we are going to read the story again to notice how CJ is feeling and how his feelings might change across the story.

Figure 5.2
Ms. Hadreas's Planning Template for a Story Explore of *Last Stop on Market Street*

Ms. Hadreas: Readers, there are lots of times in this book where CJ feels something. On our chart we recorded, "CJ closes his eyes and feels the magic" *(pointing to the Open Notice and Wonder chart and circling this noticing using an orange pen)* (Figure 5.3). Today we are going to visit this story again to think more about your noticing and to explore CJ's feelings. Have you ever felt like that, when you felt the magic? What does it feel like?

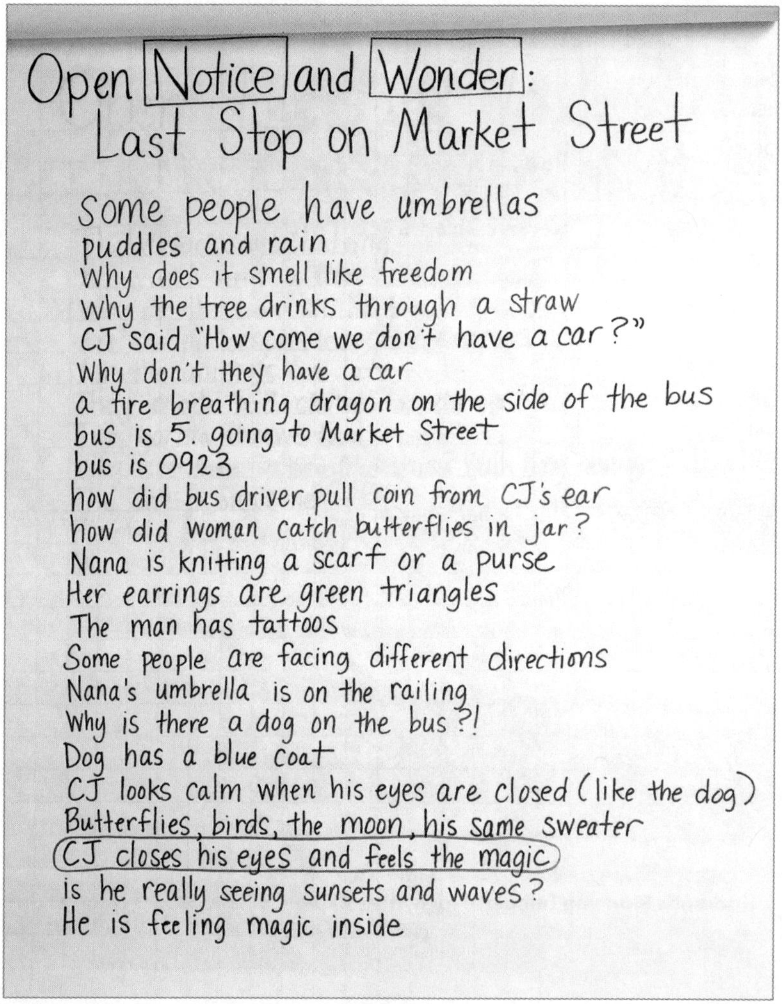

Open [Notice] and [Wonder]:
    Last Stop on Market Street

Some people have umbrellas
puddles and rain
Why does it smell like freedom
Why the tree drinks through a straw
CJ said "How come we don't have a car?"
Why don't they have a car
a fire breathing dragon on the side of the bus
bus is 5. going to Market Street
bus is 0923
how did bus driver pull coin from CJ's ear
how did woman catch butterflies in jar?
Nana is knitting a scarf or a purse
Her earrings are green triangles
The man has tattoos
Some people are facing different directions
Nana's umbrella is on the railing
Why is there a dog on the bus?!
Dog has a blue coat
CJ looks calm when his eyes are closed (like the dog)
Butterflies, birds, the moon, his same sweater
CJ closes his eyes and feels the magic
is he really seeing sunsets and waves?
He is feeling magic inside

Figure 5.3
Ms. Hadreas marks the Open Notice and Wonder Chart for the Story Explore

Mako:	It feels like you are able to dance.

Reem:	Like using your imagination.

Ms. Hadreas:	Yes! Just like Mako and Reem are doing, we want to pay attention to what characters do and say and how they feel. Let's go back to before CJ felt the magic. Did he feel like this the whole story? Let's notice what CJ is saying or doing and how he is feeling. Here at the beginning of the story, how is CJ feeling, and how do you know?

Ms. Hadreas turns to the first pages of the book to start this Story Explore read from the beginning.

Dylan:	He's happy because he skipped down the stairs. He learned about God at church.

Ms. Hadreas:	*(Turns the page)* On this page, CJ is asking, "Nana, how come we don't got a car?" How do you think CJ is feeling right now?

Natasha:	He is feeling sad because he doesn't have a car.

Ms. Hadreas:	Anyone want to add on to that feeling?

Sulamite:	Disappointed. He is mad he doesn't have a car and is sad at the same time.

Olivia:	He doesn't have enough money for a car, or maybe Nana doesn't have a license.

Ms. Hadreas:	*(Reads the next page)* So now Nana and CJ get on the bus. I'm wondering, do you think they know people on the bus? How might CJ be feeling?

Satchel:	*CJ is surprised when the bus driver does that magic trick!*

Ms. Hadreas:	Now CJ is wondering why they have to go here after church when his friends don't have to go anywhere. How do you think CJ is feeling now?
Jorge:	He is angry because he wanted to do something else.
Sulamite:	Upset. He always has to go on the bus.
Ms. Hadreas:	*(Reads the next page where two boys with a music player get on the bus)* On this page those boys have a music player and CJ doesn't. How is CJ feeling? What do you think?
Sulamite:	He is really sad because he wants one.
Ms. Hadreas:	Has there ever been a time you wanted something but weren't able to get it? Whisper to a neighbor, say, "One time . . ." *(As pairs of students share their thinking, Ms. Hadreas kneels to listen to their ideas.)*

Ms. Hadreas is taking this opportunity to help students make connections between CJ's feelings in the story and their own feelings and life experiences. She wants to translate this feeling of being sad about not having something into a deeper examination of socioeconomic status and poverty at a later time, so this is a good moment for making connections to her students' lives in a relatable way.

Ms. Hadreas:	*(Bringing students back together)* Who can tell me something, like CJ, they wish they had but couldn't get?
Frankie:	I wanted a dog, but my parents didn't want to get one. I felt sad.
Millie:	I wanted a cat! But my parents said no. I was sad, too.
Ms. Hadreas:	I can hear that people feel sad when they could not get something they wanted. Remember what happens next, that the guitar player starts plucking his strings and beginning to sing? *(Reads the next page)* Now we are back to the page

where CJ closes his eyes and feels the magic. Is he still sad, or have his feelings changed? What do you think?

Mako: He is feeling the magic. His feelings are changing. He is calm.

Khaled: Yes, he looks calm. His face looks happy and he is smiling.

Ms. Hadreas: It seems his feelings are changing. Let's finish and watch his feelings. *(Reads the next page)* How is CJ feeling as he gets off the bus and walks through the neighborhood with Nana?

Dylan: He's happy! I know because he jumped off the bus!

Mako: I jump when I am happy!

Julyssa: Or excited!

Ms. Hadreas reads the next page, which shows CJ and Nana walking through an urban landscape. Her goal is to support students to continue to notice the range of emotions CJ is experiencing across the story.

Sulamite: But then he gets disgusted, because the neighborhood is dirty.

Olivia: And he's holding Nana's hand and he is scared.

Ms. Hadreas: *(Turns to and reads the next page)* Yes, he has so many feelings! How does he feel now, on this page, and what might have helped his feelings change?

Julyssa: He's excited! His grandma helped him. She showed him the rainbow.

Ms. Hadreas: Turn and tell a neighbor, who helps you feel better in your life? *(As students talk with one another, Ms. Hadreas sits beside a few pairs to listen in.)* Who would like to report out what you and your neighbor discussed? Share your thoughts about who helps you see things in a new way or feel better in your life.

Ms. Hadreas pauses here to connect this turning point in the story, when CJ's feelings turn positive thanks in large part to Nana's comments and wisdom, to experiences students might have had in their lives. She knows that making text-to-self connections is not only a powerful way to deepen students' comprehension of the story but also an effective strategy for nurturing a positive learning community in her classroom.

Jorge: My dad helps me. He talks to me and tells me to breathe in and out.

Lulu: My mom. She helps me because she held my hand when I got my flu shot.

Reem: My grandma helps me, like CJ. My grandma, well I call her Mimi, she rubs my back when I am sad.

Ms. Hadreas: Here at the end of the story they are in this place *(pointing to the illustration of the soup kitchen line entrance)* and as they enter, CJ tells Nana, "I'm glad we came." How is he feeling now?

Mako: He's happy! He has been here before and he knows people.

Ms. Hadreas turns to the last page, where Nana and CJ are helping in the soup kitchen.

Ms. Hadreas: Let's remember, what are Nana and CJ doing here?

Khaled: Maybe they are earning money to buy a car.

Sulamite: They are helping serve the food.

Ms. Hadreas: Why might they be helping and serving? How does CJ feel now? What do you think?

Sulamite: I think they are cooking with other people. He looks like he feels helpful and glad.

Julyssa: They are giving people in their community something to eat. CJ and Nana are poor too, but they are helping other people who are their neighbors.

Satchel: He might feel a little bored because he's working, and it isn't time to play.

Frankie: CJ is happy, because he enjoys spending time with Nana and the people he knows.

Throughout the discussion, Ms. Hadreas charts the feeling words mentioned by her students, so that at the end of the read-aloud there is a long list (Figure 5.4). After finishing the book, she reads the whole list of words with her students, expressing amazement at the number of feelings CJ experienced across the story. Ms. Hadreas shares the students' observation that Nana helped CJ transition from bad feelings to good ones, especially when she helped him notice the rainbow above the gritty city skyline.

Eager to have students make personal connections to CJ's range of feelings, Ms. Hadreas reads the charted list of feelings words with her students and then prompts them, saying, "I would like for you to think about a time when you had one of these feelings. Think: What were you doing and who were you with? Think about a time when you felt that way. Close your eyes like CJ and notice: What was happening? Who was there? Was there someone like Nana who helped you think about something and maybe feel better? Can you picture who was there and what was happening? When you're ready, turn and share your thinking with a neighbor." As students begin to share their noticings in pairs, Ms. Hadreas jots a note to herself about a thought for an Idea Investigation activity about feelings to help her students continue to explore this important topic in a thoughtful way after the three read-aloud experiences. We will share this investigation in Chapter 6.

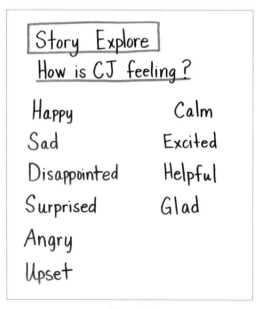

Figure 5.4
Ms. Hadreas's Class Feelings Chart from Story Explore of *Last Stop on Market Street*

Math Lens in a Primary-Grade Classroom: *Last Stop on Market Street*

After the Open Notice and Wonder read and the Story Explore read, Ms. Hadreas's students are deep into the story context of *Last Stop on Market Street*. The story has become a shared experience in their classroom that is shaping how the community talks with one another. Students can be heard referring to CJ, Nana, and the other book characters throughout the school day: "I'm feeling the magic like CJ!" "I rode the bus this weekend, like CJ and Nana." "I was grumpy this weekend, until I went to the park and saw my friends . . . like when CJ felt better from seeing people in his community."

Ms. Hadreas is excited to read the story again, for a third time, and to invite children to think as mathematicians. After listening to students discuss the ways people in CJ's day influenced his feelings during the Story Explore read, she wants to delve more deeply into the theme of *community* in this story. She keeps thinking about how Frankie said, "CJ is happy, because he enjoys spending time with Nana and the people he knows." She thinks about CJ's community, made up of Nana and the people on the bus and in the soup kitchen, and how these people shape his views and beliefs, as well as who he is and who he is becoming as a person. One way to think within this story as a mathematician is to pay attention to how many people are in CJ's community. This focus deepens students' understanding of the story and the importance of community. Ms. Hadreas sketches some notes on the focused read planning template (Figure 5.5). She also jots ideas on sticky notes and places them within the book (Figure 5.6). As we drop in on their discussion, if you have access to a copy of *Last Stop on Market Street*, it may be helpful and interesting to follow along with Ms. Hadreas and her students.

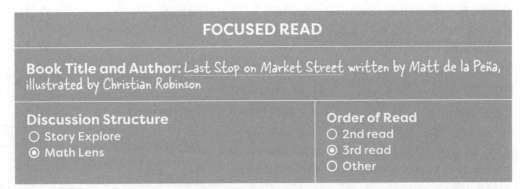

FOCUSED READ

Book Title and Author: Last Stop on Market Street written by Matt de la Peña, illustrated by Christian Robinson

Discussion Structure
○ Story Explore
◉ Math Lens

Order of Read
○ 2nd read
◉ 3rd read
○ Other

Making Connections
Which ideas from the first Open Notice and Wonder read (and/or the Story Explore or Math Lens read) do I want to pursue? Why?

- Students noticed many times in the story CJ feels something.
- Students discussed CJ's feelings and how they changed across the story.
- The people CJ meets shape his feelings. I want students to keep track of the people 1) to practice and share counting and recording strategies, 2) to develop cardinality, and 3) to see the quantity of people in CJ's day and think about the theme of community.

What portion of the story will I reread?

- ○ Entire story
- ○ Part of the story
- ◉ Revisit illustration(s)

Where Might We Pause and Why?

Page (Description)	Story Explore or Math Lens Question/Prompt
P. 5 (Church doors)	How many people do you see? Show us!
P. 8 (How come we don't got a car)	How many people do you see?
P. 12 (Having just boarded the bus)	How many people do you see?
P. 14 (Four people on bus, sitting in a row)	How many people do you see? How do you see them?
P. 28 (In line to enter soup kitchen)	How many people do you see?
P. 30 (In the soup kitchen)	How many people do you see? How do you see them?

How Will I Launch the Story?
I will refer to the charted ideas about CJ's feelings from the Story Explore discussion and invite students to revisit the story as mathematicians to notice and count the people in CJ's community. I will ask for ideas about how to keep track to make sure everyone has a way to begin.

Figure 5.5
Ms. Hadreas's Planning Template for Math Lens Read of *Last Stop on Market Street*

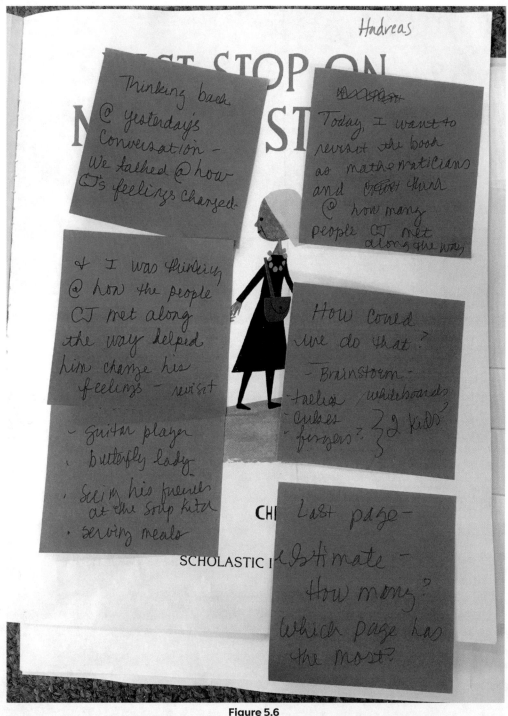

Figure 5.6
Ms. Hadreas's Copy of *Last Stop on Market Street* with Sticky Notes for Planning the Math Lens Read

Ms. Hadreas: Mathematicians, as I was thinking back to yesterday when we read *Last Stop on Market Street* (*running her hand over the charted ideas from the Open Notice and Wonder read with the circled idea for the Story Explore read*), I was thinking about the things that we noticed and wondered about with CJ and his Nana and about the conversation from our Story Explore of CJ's changing feelings. Something you thought about, that really stuck with me, was how you noticed the different feelings CJ experienced (*pointing to the feelings chart*) and the ways his feelings changed across the story. I was thinking about how the people CJ met along the way shaped his feelings and how Nana helped him see things differently. Like the butterfly lady who made him happy! And the guitar guy—oh, he changed everything!

Olivia: That was when CJ was feeling the magic (*stretching out her arms and closing her eyes like CJ does in the illustration*).

Ms. Hadreas: Yes! (*Mimicking the student and holding out her hands and closing her eyes*) Let's all feel the magic like CJ!

Students join in, spreading their arms wide and closing their eyes, "I feel the magic!"

Ms. Hadreas: I am thinking about the people in his community in the soup kitchen where he was working (*holding up and showing the soup kitchen illustration*) (Figure 5.7). When we discussed this part of the story, you had me thinking about communities of people and how people work together and how those people shape how we feel. And I thought to myself, today I want to revisit this book as mathematicians. To look at this book with math eyes and think about how many people CJ meets along the way, how many people CJ has in his community, and what community means. What ideas do you have for how we could notice and keep track of the people in CJ's community? (*Looking to Millie who is beginning to share*) How could we keep track?

Millie:	We could write down their names or a description of them. Like, *Nana*. Or *Guitar Guy*.
Ms. Hadreas:	*(Repeating Millie's idea)* We could write down a word that is their name or who they are. What else?
Frankie:	We could draw a line every time he meets a new person *(gesturing drawing a line in the air)*.
Ms. Hadreas:	Is that line a ten stick or a tally mark?
Frankie:	A tally mark.
Maggie:	What is a tally mark?
Ms. Hadreas:	*(Turning to Frankie)* Can you describe to Maggie and the rest of us what you mean by a tally mark?
Frankie:	A tally mark is a line that counts as one; like you do not have time to draw out a whole thing, you can just make a mark and that means one.

Ms. Hadreas takes a moment to encourage discussion about the different ways mathematicians keep track or record their count. She noticed earlier in the day that students were exploring different ways to record their count during Counting Collections (another mathematical routine in their classroom). She is glad Maggie asked about tally marks and Frankie shared his thinking. Listening to Maggie and Frankie, Ms. Hadreas could hear how students were making sense of mathematical representations, and the class could work together through this discussion to surface, define, and clarify different ways of recording.

Ms. Hadreas:	OK, so we might write a word for someone or draw a tally mark. What else?
Avery:	A circle.
Khaled:	Or, you could write like *1, 2, 3 . . .* every time there is a new person.

Ms. Hadreas:	So, writing numbers in a running total with the number that comes next.
Reem:	What number do we start with? I think we start with two already because of Nana and CJ.
Ms. Hadreas:	You're thinking of beginning with two.
Fana:	No, not two, just one for Nana, CJ isn't in his own community.
Avery:	Yes, he is!
Ms. Hadreas:	It sounds like we have differing ideas about how to begin counting. That is OK. We can have discussions along the way, as we read, because we might have different numbers. Decide how *you* want to keep track, and it will be exciting if we have different ideas!
Zuri:	I have one more way! We can use a ten-frame.
Ms. Hadreas:	Say more about your thinking.
Zuri:	Well, I can put the ten-frame under the document camera and keep track with counters. We can add another ten-frame if there are more than ten people.
Ms. Hadreas:	OK, gather the materials and do that! *(Turning to the class)* We hear people are going to use a variety of ways to keep track— tally marks, circles, counting on, ten-frames. Does everyone feel like they have a way to begin and to keep track of the people in CJ's day—the people he shares experiences with, the people he works with, the people he learns with and from?

With clipboards, plain paper, and pencils, students gather around on the carpet, ready to begin. Children begin to chat about how many they are going to start with: "I'm starting with one. Just Nana." "I'm starting with two. Nana and CJ."

Ms. Hadreas: We aren't going to read every word of the story; we'll skim the pages to notice people. *(Opening to the first page)* Here are CJ and Nana walking to the bus stop. How many people do you see? People in our room might count differently and that is OK! *(Turning the pages and narrating)* Oh, here are his friends Colby and Miguel from church, you can count them if you like *(turning the pages again while students are recording).*

Dylan: The bus driver!

Ms. Hadreas: The bus driver, nice! Yes, CJ's community *(pointing to the illustration inside the bus with people sitting on long benches beneath the windows).* How many people do you see? How do you see them? Whisper to a neighbor! I hear six, I hear seven, eight! Who can share their thinking?

Satchel: I saw eight. I saw one, two, three, and then another person. And then five, six, seven.

Jorge: But we already counted CJ, Nana, and the bus driver, and we do not count them again.

Ms. Hadreas: What do you think about this? Some mathematicians are counting all the people on the bus. Some mathematicians think we may have already counted some of these people.

Sulamite: It is five. Because there are eight people on the bus, but then I crossed off three because we already counted Nana, CJ, and the bus driver.

Lulu: Yeah, I agree.

Natasha: I'm keeping track of my totals. I have fifteen people!

Zuri: I have fifteen, too.

Ms. Hadreas: Zuri, can you tell us how you're keeping track? How you count fifteen?

Zuri:	I am still using ten-frames. The ones we have right here *(pointing to laminated ten-frames near a math supply station)*. Every time I count a person, I add a counter *(holding up a plastic circle counter)*. I filled up one ten-frame and then part of another *(running her finger along the top row of the ten-frame, which is covered with counters)*. So that is 10 and then . . . 1, 2, 3, 4, 5 more so far.
Ms. Hadreas:	OK, add on to your total in a way that matches your thinking. Mathematicians, so exciting! We may not think the same—that is OK.
Frankie:	The dog!
Reem:	Does the dog count?
Frankie:	Does the dog count? Yeah, it does!

Ms. Hadreas appreciates the way students are actualizing their mathematical agency. Students have choice about how to count and what to count. Listening to students make their own decisions reminds her there is no "right" way to count; rather, it is students' reasoning that is of value.

Ms. Hadreas:	Some people are feeling like counting the dog. You decide! Do you want to count the dog? Is the dog part of CJ's community? *(Turning the pages)*
Sulamite:	The boys with the headphones!
Mako:	There is a new person! *(Pointing to the man on the bus)*
Khaled:	Wait, *no*, that is the guitar man. He took his hat off!
Dylan:	His hat is on the floor of the bus so people can put coins in his hat. So, we already counted him!
Reem:	Is that a new person? *(Pointing to a woman)*

Frankie: Yeah!

Khaled: No! She has the same patterned skirt. We saw her on the bus earlier—sitting next to the guitar man!

Ms. Hadreas: I didn't notice her before. I see her now! We're helping each other notice new things in these illustrations! *(Turning to the last page)* And finally, let's study the soup kitchen where his community comes together, where there are so many people in CJ's life. As you look at this illustration *(holding up the illustration for everyone to see)*, let's notice or estimate how many people there are. Talk with your neighbor, how many people do you see? How do you see them?

Figure 5.7
Soup Kitchen Illustration from *Last Stop on Market Street*

Children can be overheard explaining their strategies to one another. Ms. Hadreas kneels beside students to listen to how they are counting. She can hear students counting by ones, seeing groups, and counting on. Another student has started using a ten-frame with plastic coins to keep track. It is a good opportunity to hear the range of ways students are counting.

Ms. Hadreas: *(Pulling the group back together)* I can hear you counting in so many different ways! Let's hear a few more strategies. Lulu?

Lulu: I counted by ones. I counted one, two, three, four *(beginning in the lower left-hand corner of the pages and pointing to each person)*.

Avery: I counted by twos. I said 2, 4, 6, 8, 10, 12, 14, and then I counted these 2 down here *(pointing to two more people in the illustration)*.

Jorge: I want to add on to Avery's way. I counted by twos, too. And then I counted by threes down here *(pointing to some people in the bottom right-hand corner table)*.

Natasha: Many of the people on the bus were in the line at the soup kitchen, and now they are at the tables in this soup kitchen.

Ms. Hadreas: You're noticing that some of the people on the bus and in the line are also at these tables.

Sulamite: And some of them are standing right with CJ and Nana.

Satchel: *Wow*! CJ has a big community!

Mako: He has *much much much* community!

The goals for this discussion are to keep track of the people in CJ's day, to practice and share counting and recording strategies, and to think more deeply about the quantity of people in the story, with an emphasis on community. Ms. Hadreas pauses for a moment to think about how to bring the discussion to a close for today, highlighting the big ideas that have emerged, and setting the class up for an extension discussion that would happen the following day.

Ms. Hadreas: He does have *much* community! So many people shared this day with CJ! Today, as mathematicians, you decided how to keep track of the people in CJ's world. You kept track using tally marks or circles, you counted on, and you used a ten-frame. There are many ways to keep track when you are counting. What we could see, over time, was that CJ met many people in his day. And that CJ has a *big* community. People in our community shape how we feel, how we think, and we also shape how the people in our day feel and think. People in our community bring us joy. You bring joy to your community. There is joy within CJ's community. In the coming days, we will return to this story and think more about the theme of community. I invite you to notice how many people are in your day and think about who you are in your community. Nice thinking, mathematicians!

Planning for a Focused Read

Before moving on to an example of focused reads in an intermediate-grade classroom, let's pause to describe how to plan for focused Story Explore or Math Lens reads (see Figure 5.8). When planning for a focused read, we tend to begin by carefully considering the ideas that emerged during the first Open Notice and Wonder read (if an Open Notice and Wonder read has occurred previously). Glancing over the charted ideas from the first read, you might ask yourself, "What did my students think about in the first read? Which of their ideas do I want to pursue? Why?" For example, are there particular literary noticings about story elements such as plot, setting, or character traits that are current areas of focus during reading time? Or perhaps there are mathematical noticings that would be interesting to think through more together, such as ideas that connect to the mathematical concepts or practices your students are currently studying. Additionally, students may have mathematical wonderings that the class would benefit from discussing in more depth, or connections between story events and children's lives. Students' noticings and wonderings provide opportunities to explore their ideas in more depth.

FOCUSED READ

Book Title and Author

Discussion Structure	Order of Read
○ Story Explore	○ 2nd read
○ Math Lens	○ 3rd read
	○ Other

Making Connections
Which ideas from the first Open Notice and Wonder read (and/or the Story Explore or Math Lens read) do I want to pursue? Why?

What portion of the story will I reread?
○ Entire story
○ Part of the story
○ Revisit illustration(s)

Where Might We Pause and Why?

Page (Description)	Story Explore or Math Lens Question/Prompt

How Will I Launch the Story?

Figure 5.8
Planning Template for Focused Reads
(Found in Appendix C)

Next, we think through which portion of the story to reread and why. You may choose to reread the entire story, a portion of the story, or return to one or more illustrations through a focused discussion or picture walk. You might select the portion of the story that will best support your students to think more deeply about the literary or mathematical ideas you want to focus upon and further discuss. In the previous vignettes, Ms. Hadreas chose to review the entire book through a picture walk and discussion for the Story Explore, but she chose to pause only on selected illustrations for the Math Lens. For the Story Explore, she chose to review the entire story because she wanted students to track CJ's feelings as they evolved and changed across their journey, whereas for the Math Lens read, her goal for the discussion was to support students to count the people in CJ's community. Ms. Hadreas believed she could best do this by skimming through the pages, pausing on particular pages to highlight CJ's community on the bus and in the soup kitchen. Also, because it was the third time visiting the book, she believed that the students had come to know the story in depth already.

Once you've decided which portion of the story to reread, you're ready to jot down a few notes about where you may pause and why. We sketch in notes on the planning template to make sure our ideas are clear. On the template, there are rows where you can note the page(s) where you plan to pause and also what questions or prompts you may use to spur students' discussion. One thing we have come to learn about children's literature is that book pages are not typically numbered. Therefore, we often note to ourselves a short description of the page and place a sticky note on that page to mark it as a pausing spot. This portion of planning is helpful in anticipating where we may pause; however, we also remain flexible and adaptive to what we hear from students in the moment. There may end up being important places to pause that we did not anticipate when planning!

Finally, consider how you want to launch the read. What might you say or ask children as you invite them back into this story as readers and/or mathematicians? We try to be explicit in telling students if they are approaching this story as readers or as mathematicians and that when we read with different lenses, we notice different things. In her Story Explore read, for example, Ms. Hadreas began with the page of *Last Stop on Market Street* where CJ was shown "feeling the magic" of the music, starting with a quick discussion of what that feeling was like and then going to the beginning of the book to track his feelings across the story.

Although many planning elements are the same for a Math Lens and a Story Explore read, it is important to also consider what is different between these two discussion structures and why. Let's take a look at a few content area–specific considerations, or essentials, of planning for a Math Lens and Story Explore read.

Math Lens Essentials

A Math Lens read is a playful time to enjoy stories as mathematicians—to explore mathematical ideas and questions in an engaging and thoughtful way. During this type of read, we invite students to enjoy a story with a math lens! Approaching stories as mathematicians is thrilling, and it is something we do not tend to get enough time for in our classrooms.

We keep some special considerations in mind when planning and facilitating a Math Lens read. When planning, we begin by studying the mathematical ideas students have shared in the previous reads. What did students notice and wonder as mathematicians during the Open Notice and Wonder read? Or, if you have already facilitated a Story Explore read, how might mathematical noticings and wonderings have appeared or evolved? What new mathematical ideas may have surfaced?

Next, we ask ourselves which of these ideas we want to pursue in a Math Lens read and why. You might choose, for example, to pursue an idea that is connected to concepts or practices you are currently studying. The story context may provide a powerful opportunity to see and understand the mathematical ideas and practices you're studying in a new way. For example, if your students are beginning to learn about multiplication and you want them to have an opportunity to see groups of groups, you might choose to focus on illustrations in the story *One Is a Snail, Ten Is a Crab* (Sayre and Sayre 2006). There are many illustrations in this story that encourage children to engage in sensemaking discussion about groups. We especially love the two-page spread in this book that shows on one side four crabs with ten legs each and on the other side, ten dogs each with four legs (Figure 5.9). Young mathematicians can count all the crab legs by ones (or count by tens) to notice and prove that four groups of ten is forty legs. Students may write equations to match the illustration such as $10 + 10 + 10 + 10 = 40$ or $4 \times 10 = 40$. You could discuss how and why both of these equations are true and articulate where each part of the equation is in the illustration. This is a nice opportunity to use the question as refrain "How might you use the illustrations to show your thinking?" (See Appendix B.) Children can point to the crab legs in the illustration to prove that 4 groups of 10 is 40 and/or that 10 groups of 4 is 40. As one first-grade child said, pointing to each crab leg and counting by ones, "See here it is, 1, 2, 3, 4 . . 39, 40. There are forty legs on these crabs!" Or as one third-grade student said, placing his hand on each crab and skip counting by tens, "There are ten, twenty, thirty, forty. Four tens is forty. You can see it right here on the crabs!"

Figure 5.9
Illustration from *One Is a Snail, Ten Is a Crab*

Also, a young mathematician may count all the dog legs by 1s, or count by 4s, to see that 10 groups of 4 is the same as 40. Similarly, children may write equations to match the illustration, such as $4 + 4 + 4 + 4 + 4 + 4 + 4 + 4 + 4 + 4 = 40$ or $10 \times 4 = 40$. Using both of these illustrations (of the crabs and the dogs) at the same time, you might engage in a true-or-false number equation, posing the equation $4 \times 10 = 10 \times 4$ and invite children to use the illustrations to prove if this equation is true or false! The context of this story, and the captivating illustrations, help support young mathematicians to build on what they understand about addition to think about multiplication.

You might also choose to think more about an interesting mathematical idea that lies outside your current studies but is genuinely interesting to your young mathematicians. For example, after reading *One Is a Snail, Ten Is a Crab*, a class of third-grade students wondered, "How many leg combinations could we make from the animals in this story?" They spun off on their own investigation (during choice time), generating pages and pages of equations inspired by the combinations of animal legs in the story. They made a chart that showed all the animals in the story and how many legs each animal had (a snail has one foot!), and then drew the combinations of animals with matching equations. Although this activity did not map onto their current studies within their classroom curriculum, it was very engaging to these young mathematicians. It reminds us of Kassia Wedekind's noticing, "My question is not always the question students want to think about." This was the students' question and their idea. They ran with it for days! This example illustrates the power of stories as playful places to nurture curiosity and joy for mathematics, broadly, as well as to play mathematically for mathematics' sake. For this reason, we encourage you to remain open to pursuing mathematical ideas that are related concepts or practices you're currently studying as well as mathematics beyond the ideas you're studying.

Finally, during the enactment of the Math Lens read-aloud discussion, we have found it is important to stay focused on the mathematics. It can be tempting to pursue other interesting ideas that may emerge (as we do in an Open Notice and Wonder). However, a Math Lens discussion is about delving into the story as mathematicians. From our experiences facilitating Math Lens reads, we have noticed that students' thinking as mathematicians will be inextricably connected to the story. This is exciting! We want to support students to leverage the story context to think mathematically. In the upcoming vignette, you will read how Ms. Burris stays focused on students' mathematical ideas in a Math Lens read-aloud. Her questions are aimed to help students explore mathematical ideas in the story, asking about portions of cake the animals eat in *The Lion's Share* and engaging in sense making about halves, fourths, and eighths.

Story Explore Essentials

The key to planning and enacting an engaging Story Explore read is to keep focused on one or two story ideas or topics. When planning for a Story Explore read, we keep three factors in mind: (1) teaching points in reading instruction, (2) students' interests, and (3) features of the book itself. First let's consider teaching points. If in reading workshop the class is focusing on a particular reading comprehension strategy, we might choose a Story Explore read-aloud accordingly. For example, if you are currently exploring character traits and development, you might consider focusing the Story Explore on character in a book like *Grumpy Bird* (Tankard 2016), as Bird's feelings are central to the story and seem to change over time, from grumpy to cheerful (or at least *not* grumpy) thanks to his group of persistent and determined friends. We really enjoy reading *Stack the Cats* (Ghahremani 2018) with a focus on prediction. This story provides several startling opportunities to pause and ask students what they think might happen next and why (Figure 5.10). For the strategy of retelling or summarizing, *Dog's Colorful Day* (Dodd 2003) provides an excellent opportunity to recall the sequence of how Dog got each of its ten colorful spots. For visualizing, *Jabari Jumps* (Cornwall 2017) allows us to think about perspective and what it must feel and look like to be so high up and to have to jump!

Four cats teeter.

Five cats totter.

Figure 5.10
Illustration from *Stack the Cats*

Another factor is student interest, particularly if you've done an Open Notice and Wonder read-aloud and students engaged in a lively debate or discussion about a theme or topic in the book. We found one group of students focused on the idea of friendship in *Square Cat* (Schoonmaker 2011), where Eula's friends do everything they can to help her feel better about being square. Given the relevant nature of this theme to school and to life in general, we thought it well worth the time to explore together with students, asking questions about their actions as friends and the ways they tried to help Eula feel better.

At other times, a feature of the book itself warrants further attention, as each work of children's literature emphasizes plot, character, setting, dialogue, and vocabulary in different and interesting ways. *Circle Square Moose* (Bingham 2014), for example, contains multiple visual perspectives and different points of view (including the animals escaping from the pages of the book). In *The Most Magnificent Thing* (Spires 2014), the word *magnificent* is crucial to the story. We have helped students discuss what they think this word might mean in connection to what the girl was trying to build, coming up with a working definition of *magnificent* in the process. *Small Medium Large* (Jenkins 2011) also utilizes interesting vocabulary, in this case a range of size-related vocabulary worth exploring, with words from *tiny* and *miniscule* to *gigantic* and *enormous*. *The Snowy Day* (Keats 1976) describes a sequence of events for the boy in the snow worth recalling after reading, as many of these might relate to students' own life experiences. Whether the central focus comes from your teaching points, student interest, or the text itself, the key is to focus Story Explore read-aloud and discussion on just those one or two ideas.

Once you've determined a focus, a quick planning sketch is the next step. Where will you want to pause in the story, and what questions or prompts will you provide to help students explore the key ideas you've chosen for your focus? We like to jot these questions on sticky notes and place them in the book as a reminder while reading. When you have finished the read-aloud, what prompts might you provide to help students continue exploring key ideas through discussion? Having a lively discussion after reading, even if the discussion is brief, is an excellent way to synthesize ideas and to extend students' thinking and learning. Finally, looking across the lesson sketch, what will you say and do to launch the Story Explore read? If the purpose is to practice a reading comprehension strategy taught during reading time, such as predicting or visualizing, mentioning that strategy before reading helps students make connections. If the focus is drawn from a charted Open Notice and Wonder idea, referring to that chart and then to the corresponding page of the book is a great way to start. If the focus is from the text itself, we find it helpful to name the text feature and show a page (or the front cover) where that feature is prominent. It's important to keep in mind that the launch is where you set the purpose for the focused Story Explore read and help activate and build students' background knowledge, getting them ready to engage with the focus idea and the story.

Read-Alouds: What Order and Why?

There is not a fixed order for focused read-alouds. You might choose to follow an Open Notice and Wonder with a Story Explore and then a Math Lens read, or vice versa. The order of the reads is flexible and depends on what will best support students' thinking about the literary and mathematics you, and they, want to study. For example, engaging students in a Story Explore read before a Math Lens read often allows students to delve more deeply into the story context. And specifically, if the comprehension strategy of prediction is your focus, you'll want to have the Story Explore read first so that students can discuss and predict story events as they unfold for the first time!

You'll notice that the order of the vignettes in this chapter is Open Notice and Wonder, into a Story Explore, and finally a Math Lens. Our experiences using *Last Stop on Market Street* and *The Lion's Share* with students and teachers taught us that it was powerful to read these stories in this order. Beginning with an Open Notice and Wonder read got our community into the story; following that with a Story Explore read and discussions took us further within the story context and allowed us to think as mathematicians deeply within the context. But we want to be clear that other sequences work equally well for different books and areas of focus. We encourage you to play with order and see what you learn!

Here are a couple of examples of books that we might explore using a different focused-read order. *Square Cat*, the book about Eula the cat that wants to be round and is sad to be square, has a plot twist near the end. This twist lends itself to a focus on predicting story events, so we would introduce *Square Cat* with a Story Explore focused read first. We would likely do an Open Notice and Wonder read second, to provide an opportunity for students to identify story details and pose questions about Eula the cat, her features, why she is upset, and how her friends try to help her. We would focus on a Math Lens read third, as Eula the cat's problems relate directly to the properties of a square; this read would build on the first two reads to look deeply at shapes and how their properties and characteristics impact the world around them.

The Most Magnificent Thing, the tale of the girl determined to build a creation she has imagined clearly in her mind, is a story of engineering that centers the mathematical practice of perseverance. With this story we might focus first on perseverance through a Math Lens read, helping students see what it looks like to be within a state of struggle and how a mathematician persists through an iterative cycle as she revises her ideas. We might then facilitate an Open Notice and Wonder read to see what else students might think about, from the girl's feelings across the story to the number of attempts she made, from her process of working through frustration to the actions of her dog assistant. We would then do a Story Explore read to focus on some of these ideas, which in our experience with this book might include examining the characteristics of what makes a thing "magnificent" and, based on this, what magnificent thing students might think of and try to create.

With both of these examples, we find it important to remember that the order of the read-alouds can vary depending on concepts, purpose, student interest, and the nature of the book itself. We also know that not every book needs to be read three times, and even if you decide to do all three read-aloud types with a book, you don't have to read the entire story and the reads don't have to be done three days in a row or even within one week. Students love revisiting familiar stories weeks or even months after being introduced to them. Our goal is to inspire students to explore math and literary ideas within the rich context of stories.

Story Explore in an Intermediate-Grade Classroom: *The Lion's Share*

Ms. Burris, amused by her students' outrage over the animals' behavior as dinner guests in *The Lion's Share*, decides to pursue this idea in the book through a focused Story Explore read of the first half of the book. A couple of the charted Open Notice and Wonder ideas that draw her attention are "I wonder why the lion is not talking" and "I notice they're cutting every half they can. I predict the lion will not get any!" Ms. Burris wants to build on these ideas, prompting her students to think about the animals and how their method for cutting the birthday cake relates to the concepts of *fair* and *equal*. As she sketches plans for this Story Explore read (Figure 5.11), her goal is to use students' engagement with these ideas in the story to help them explore these same concepts, *fair* and *equal*, from a mathematical perspective in a subsequent Math Lens read.

Ms. Burris jots down a few prompts and questions on sticky notes, placing these on pages in the first half of *The Lion's Share* to help her prepare for what she predicts will be a lively discussion. She also plans to pose some questions for discussion after the Story Explore read: "What is fair?" "What is equal?" and "How are these ideas different and the same?" This prompt will, Ms. Burris hopes, serve as a bridge to a Math Lens read exploring these same ideas mathematically.

FOCUSED READ

Book Title and Author: The Lion's Share written by Matthew McElligott

Discussion Structure	**Order of Read**
◉ Story Explore	◉ 2nd read
○ Math Lens	○ 3rd read
	○ Other

Making Connections
Which ideas from the first Open Notice and Wonder read (and/or the Story Explore or Math Lens read) do I want to pursue? Why?

We noticed that the animals at Lion's party behaved awfully! Students were outraged by how selfish the animals were and that they were rude and unfair to Ant. I want to pursue this idea of fairness and equality.

What portion of the story will I reread?

○ Entire story
◉ Part of the story
○ Revisit illustration(s)

Where Might We Pause and Why?

Page (Description)	Story Explore or Math Lens Question/Prompt
P. 5 (All arrived late)	How did the ant act, and how did she feel? How did the other animals act, and how do you think they feel?
P. 7 (Dinner party chaos)	How are the lion and ant acting, and how might they be feeling? How are the other animals acting, and what do you think of their behavior?
P. 9 (Elephant cuts cake in half)	How is the elephant acting? What does he think and do? What do you think of his actions, and what do you think will happen next?
P. 11 (Hippo cuts cake in half)	How is the hippo acting? What does she think and do? What do you think of her actions, and what do you think will happen next?
P. 15 (Disgusted animals)	How are the animals acting? What do they think of the ant? Do you think this is fair? Why or why not?

How Will I Launch the Story?

Look at the cover together. "Readers, remember how awfully the animals acted at Lion's party? What do we now know is happening in the illustration on the front cover of the book? We are going to read the first part of this story again to explore how the animals acted and whether we think they behaved or acted fairly— and what that means.

Figure 5.11
Ms. Burris's Planning Template for Story Explore of *The Lion's Share*

Ms. Burris: Readers, sometimes characters in a story act differently than we think they will or maybe how they should. In *The Lion's Share* you noticed *(pointing at the Open Notice and Wonder chart)* that most of the animals behaved awfully! Looking at the cover of the book, what do we now know is going on here?

Kazuo: The ant has nothing to pass to the lion because her piece was too small to cut. All of the other animals took waaaaay too much.

Ms. Burris: Interesting! Does anyone want to add on to what Kazuo is saying?

Ayana: Yeah, all of the other animals took too much. They kept cutting in half and half and the big pieces only left small portions.

Peder: Exactly!

Ms. Burris: I can hear you have ideas and feelings, about the characters in this story. Let's revisit the first part of this story. I want all of us to pay attention to how the animals act, how this might make us feel as readers, and how we might act and do things differently at a dinner party. Here, on this page where the ant has arrived on time and all the other animals arrive late, what do you think about how they are acting and feeling, and how do you know?

Maya: I know the ant is nervous about the party because it says "she was very nervous." And also because she gets there on time. Whenever my mom is nervous, I notice she pays close attention to time!

Roshann: She gets there on time because that is polite. But all of the other animals get there late, and that's not polite. I think maybe the lion will be mad because they're late.

Ms. Burris: Let's keep going. On this next page, what is happening?

Abby: It's terrible! The gorilla is throwing food and they're all making a mess.

Naomi: The ant is watching, and the lion isn't saying anything. Maybe he *is* mad! Why is the warthog eating the flowers? I don't think you're supposed to do that at a dinner!

Kazuo: Definitely not!

Ms. Burris: You have ideas about these animals! Now it's time for cake and the elephant helps himself first. What does he do? What do you think about what he does? And what might happen next?

Aram: He thinks about eating the whole cake, but he cuts it in half instead. Elephants are big. So, I think he could've eaten the whole thing easily all by himself.

Christian: But it's not fair. There are lots of other animals and now the cake is half gone because of the elephant. I don't think it's fair to take half of the whole dessert. If each animal does that then everything will go wrong.

Ms. Burris: What do people think about Christian's idea that taking half of the whole is not fair?

Neeku: I agree. They each took half and at the beginning that was a huge piece. It's not fair because the pieces are not the same size, even though I guess they are all half. It is kind of confusing to explain.

Ms. Burris: I like the way you're thinking and trying to explain your ideas. I also like how you're building on each other's ideas. Let's keep going! Now on this next page the hippo helps herself to some cake. Readers, what is happening here? What does the hippo do, and what do you think about what she does?

Anika: She does the same thing!

Maya: Yeah, she calls the elephant a pig, but she does the same thing and takes half of what's left! That's really mean.

Ms. Burris: Let's keep reading. *(Ms. Burris reads the next four pages.)* What happens with the cake and the other animals? How are the animals acting, and what do they think of the ant? Do you think that is fair? Why or why not? Turn and talk with your partner about what you think *(kneeling down to listen in on students' discussions).*

"They all took too much! It's not the ant's fault there was almost nothing left by the time the cake got to her. They are mean and they're blaming the ant.

"The elephant said he shared the cake but that's not really true. He took half. That's not sharing. He didn't take an equal piece."

"The warthog didn't even want her piece. She's sitting in it!"

Ms. Burris: *(Bringing the whole group back together)* As I listen to you sharing your ideas with a neighbor, I hear you talking about how the animals all took a piece and the ant ended up with a tiny crumb—so the lion got nothing. We seem to think it isn't fair, but each animal cut the cake in half, right? So, was that equal? I am wondering, what is equal and what is fair, and how are they different?

Throughout this Story Explore read, Ms. Burris charts student responses and questions, zooming in on the ideas that touch on the concepts of fair and equal (Figure 5.12). She is able to review these ideas with students, asking them to think about and discuss the differences between fair and equal, especially in the context of *The Lion's Share.* After some lively partner talk and whole-group discussion, Ms. Burris prompts her students, "I'd like all of us to continue thinking about these two concepts, fair and equal, and how they might be the same and might be different. Tomorrow we will come back with fresh ideas so that we can think about these two concepts as mathematicians. What is fair? What is equal? Are these things the same or different, and how can we make sense of them? We will return to *The Lion's Share* and explore these ideas as mathematicians."

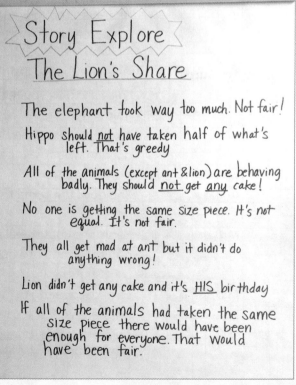

Story Explore
The Lion's Share

The elephant took way too much. Not fair!

Hippo should not have taken half of what's left. That's greedy

All of the animals (except ant & lion) are behaving badly. They should not get any cake!

No one is getting the same size piece. It's not equal. It's not fair.

They all get mad at ant but it didn't do anything wrong!

Lion didn't get any cake and it's HIS birthday

If all of the animals had taken the same size piece there would have been enough for everyone. That would have been fair.

Figure 5.12
Chart Paper from Ms. Burris's Class Discussion During the Story Explore Read of *The Lion's Share*

Math Lens in an Intermediate-Grade Classroom:
The Lion's Share

On the next day, Ms. Burris invites her students to continue thinking about *The Lion's Share*. She is excited to pursue their ideas from the Story Explore and Open Notice and Wonder discussions. To plan for the Math Lens read and discussion, Ms. Burris stepped back to look across the ideas that students had generated in the previous discussions that were captured on chart papers. Ms. Burris wanted to better understand how these young mathematicians reason about repeated halving, and how they can use (and deepen) what they know about a half and a fourth to engage in sense making about an eighth and a sixteenth. She wondered what they already understood about portions and what they were coming to understand. From the Story Explore discussion, she could hear the ways the story was helping students engage in sense making and reasoning about portions within the context of dividing the birthday cake. Specifically, she is curious to think together more about the students' emerging understanding of *fair* and *equal*. She planned to use the previous days' discussions, and the students' ideas, as the launch for this Math Lens discussion (see Figure 5.13), and in doing so, communicate to students that their questions and ideas are important and central to designing the learning in their classroom.

FOCUSED READ

Book Title and Author: The Lion's Share written by Matthew McElligott

Discussion Structure
○ Story Explore
◉ Math Lens

Order of Read
○ 2nd read
◉ 3rd read
○ Other

Making Connections
Which ideas from the first Open Notice and Wonder read (and/or the Story Explore or Math Lens read) do I want to pursue? Why?

"During the Story Explore read, you noticed the different portions of cake the animals each took and you began to raise ideas about the animals being unfair and what is fair. We discussed fair and equal and what those words mean to you. Let's visit the story again, as mathematicians, and think more about fair and equal."

What portion of the story will I reread?
○ Entire story
◉ Part of the story First half of the story—on halving.
○ Revisit illustration(s)

Figure 5.13 *(continues)*
Ms. Burris's Planning Template for Math Lens Read of *The Lion's Share*

Where Might We Pause and Why?

Page (Description)	Story Explore or Math Lens Question/Prompt
P. 9 (Elephant cuts cake in half)	"Turn and Talk: What do you notice about how the elephant cut the cake? What other ways could you cut the cake in half?"
P. 11 (Hippo cuts cake in half)	"Share what you notice about the cake. What portion did hippo take? What portion is left? How do you know?"

How Will I Launch the Story?

Revisit the charted ideas from the Open Notice and Wonder and Story Explore together. Recap salient ideas related to mathematics within the context of the story. Invite students to listen, and think, again—this time as mathematicians—with a focus on half, half of a half or fourths, fair, and equal, in relation to the animals' choices/behavior.

Figure 5.13 *(continued)*
Ms. Burris's Planning Template for Math Lens Read of *The Lion's Share*

Ms. Burris: Over last few days we have been reading *The Lion's Share* together. As we read, you shared what you noticed and what you wondered. You also shared what you noticed about the animals' behavior and began to make some conjectures about what is fair and what is equal. Here are your ideas *(pointing to the chart from the previous discussions)*.

Today, I would like to reread the first half this story again, the portion where the animals divide the cake, to think more deeply about your ideas. But, instead of sharing what you notice and wonder, or sharing what you think as a reader, we will listen to this story as mathematicians. Let's use our math lenses and get back into this story!

Ms. Burris begins reading from the beginning again. Her copy of the book has new sticky notes placed within the pages to remind her of where she plans to stop today and what questions she may ask for this read focused on mathematics. She reads the first several pages and pauses when the elephant makes the first cut of the cake.

Ms. Burris: I'd like you to turn and talk with your neighbor. What do you notice about how the elephant cut the cake? And, what other ways could *you* cut the cake in half?

As Ms. Burris glances across the pairs of students talking on the rug, she sees students making gestures in the air. Some students appear to be mimicking the elephant's slice as they show a vertical cut in the air with their hand. Other students can be seen making different cuts, such as a horizontal slice or a diagonal slice. She listens to hear students' reasoning about halves. Since she can hear that students have understanding about halves ("the cut makes two pieces that are equal and both halves together make the whole cake" and "each half is equal and the two halves together are the whole"), she decides she will not spend too much time discussing halves. She decides she will revoice a few ideas and move on to allow more time for the discussion of smaller portions—or fractions—to emerge.

Ms. Burris: *(Looking out across, and speaking to, the students gathered on the floor)* One of my favorite moments as a teacher is stepping back to observe and listen to you as mathematicians. I can hear your reasoning. For example, I hear you making mathematical statements such as "two halves make one whole" and "halves are both equal and together they are the whole." I can also see you making gestures. I saw you using gestures to show how the elephant cut the cake, and how you would cut the cake, to make two halves. I saw vertical gestures, horizontal gestures, and diagonal gestures *(modeling with her hands for each example).* I can hear you have solid reasoning about halves and I'm curious what's to come next. Let's keep going!

She continues reading. "After the elephant cut the cake in half, he passed it to the hippo who cuts down the middle, taking half of what is left." Ms. Burris pauses for discussion about half of a half. "Let's turn back to your neighbor, share what you notice about the cake. What portion did hippo take? What portion is left? How do you know?" She kneels beside students to hear their reasoning. She can hear most students clearly describe quarters, while some students are emerging in their understanding of fourths. She decides to surface their ideas to support the sense making that is happening.

Ms. Burris:	As you are reasoning about the hippo's portion of cake, I would like you to be able to hear one another's thinking and hear what questions you have.
Grace:	*(Jumping in)* I can share what Lucy, my partner, noticed. Lucy said the hippo took one quarter of the cake. She knew it was one quarter because it was a half of a half.
Ms. Burris:	Grace, I like the way you are sharing Lucy's thinking. Could either of you *(looking to both students)* share more about what you mean by "a quarter" or "a half of a half"?
Lucy:	What I mean is the elephant took half. Then the hippo took half of what was left. So that is a half of the half.
Ms. Burris:	*(Turning to the students)* What questions do you have for Lucy?
Roshann:	I see where you get the half and then the half. Where does the quarter come from?
Lucy:	A quarter is a fourth. A fourth is one piece out of four.
Ms. Burris:	I wonder if a drawing could help us? *(Handing Lucy a chart marker)*
Lucy:	Um, OK, let me see if I can draw the cake here *(draws a big rectangle)* (Figure 5.14).
Ms. Burris:	Lucy is drawing the original cake from the story.

Lucy: Yes, so here is the Lion's birthday cake. And elephant made the first cut, he cut it in half *(Using a pink chart marker, Lucy draws a vertical line down the middle of the representation of the cake.)* (Figure 5.15).

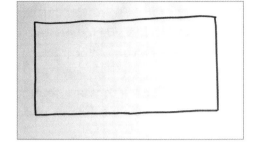

Figure 5.14
Lucy's Representation of the Birthday Cake

Ms. Burris: Questions? *(Looking to the students. Not hearing any questions, she nods to Lucy to continue.)*

Lucy: Then the hippo made the next cut. She took half of what was left. So, she took a half of a half *(using the same pink chart marker, Lucy draws a horizontal line across the representation of the cake)* (Figure 5.16).

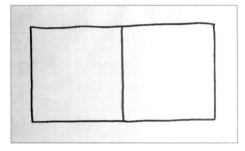

Figure 5.15
Lucy's Representation of Half of the Cake

Ms. Burris: Let's take a moment of think time to examine Lucy's drawing. Think to yourself, where do you see a half? Where do you see a half of a half? *(After a few moments of quiet thinking time)* When you're ready, turn and talk with a neighbor about your ideas.

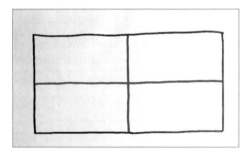

Figure 5.16
Lucy's Representation of
Half of a Half of the Cake

Ms. Burris listens to students. She can hear students describing the two halves and the half of the half. She hears:

"There is the half. And there is the half of the half."

"Yeah, I see the half you're talking about. It goes this way *(gesturing to Lucy's first half cut that was vertical).* So, the two halves are on this side *(pointing to the left)* and on this side *(pointing to the right).* We could also see it as a half on the top and a half on the bottom, if we wanted to."

"We can see that one-fourth plus one-fourth is two-fourths and we know that two-fourths is the same as one-half."

"Yes, and if the original half that the elephant took was divided in half, there would be four equal pieces. The part the hippo took is one of those pieces, it is one-fourth of the whole cake. You can see it there *(pointing to the chart paper)* and I saw it in the book."

Ms. Burris decides to bring students back together and lay the illustrations in the book alongside Lucy's representation as students reason about these portions.

Ms. Burris: Listening to you reason about halves, I want to look together at the illustration in the story and Lucy's drawing. *(Placing the pages of the book that illustrate the cake being cut in halves under the document camera and pulling the easel with Lucy's drawing to the front of the rug)* Let's look across these two representations. Talk with your neighbor to identify the halves and fourths in each representation.

Students point between the two representations. Ms. Burris can overhear students explaining:

"There is the half."

"There are the fourths."

"You can see that a fourth is a half of a half."

"So, one-fourth plus one-fourth is a half, and if you add four one-fourths together it is the whole cake."

As the class continues reading in the story, each animal continues taking half of the remaining cake. The gorilla takes a half of a fourth, the tortoise takes a half of an eighth, the warthog takes a half of a sixteenth, and so on until all that remains is a crumb for the ant to divide in two to share with the lion. With smaller portions, more complex mathematics emerges and students begin generating observations and questions, such as:

> "I notice the tortoise cut the half in half again. I know that a half of a half is a fourth. And I know you can cut that portion in half. But I don't know what a half of a fourth is called? It seems like it would have something with an eight."

> "A fourth written as a percent is 25% but you can't divide that in half. I mean, I don't think you can divide it evenly in half because it isn't an even number. So, I wonder, can you show a half of a fourth in percent?"

> "Yeah, I agree, I know there's a decimal for half and that's .5 and for a fourth that's .25 but I don't know if there's a decimal for an eighth. I don't know what that would be."

> "I wonder if you can cut something in half forever? It turns into crumbs in this story, but can you really cut in half and in half and in half—like with a microscope and the tiniest pieces? What is the tiniest piece of cake possible? What is the tiniest piece of something else possible?"

This Math Lens discussion is focused upon students' ideas about portions, using the story as a context to support reasoning and sense making about halves and halving in complex ways. Students refer to the characters, their actions, and the illustrations to generate new mathematical ideas and questions. At the point in the story when the ant receives a tiny crumb to divide in half for herself and the lion, students begin to erupt, repeating their idea from the Story Explore read, "*That's* not fair!" This time, with even deeper conviction. They dig further into discussion about the animals' bad behavior and greed, which are infuriating to some students. Their arguments about fair and equal are steeped in mathematical statements.

"It is not equal! It is not equal *because* each half was a half of the part that was left!"

"A half of a half is not the same as a half of a whole!"

In contrast, some students believed that the portions *were* fair based upon the animals' sizes, "The elephant should have the largest piece, it is biggest! And, the ant is the smallest."

"I disagree, what about the lion?!"

A lively mathematical debate arises with arguments about what is fair, what is equal, and what is and is not just in the context of this story. Ms. Burris is thrilled! As she listens, she jots a note to herself for a follow-up Idea Investigation the next day, inspired by quotes she could hear from students, "How would you divide the cake? Is fair the same as equal? Why?" We will describe her Idea Investigation with *The Lion's Share* in the next chapter.

Reflection and Discussion Questions

As you finish reading this chapter, here are some reflection questions for you to consider on your own or with colleagues:

1. As I practice planning for and facilitating different read-alouds and discussions with different goals, how do my questions differ from one discussion to the next? What types of questions do I tend to ask? What is a good next step for growing my practice as a questioner?

2. As I experience different read-aloud approaches (Open Notice and Wonder, Math Lens, Story Explore), what are some possibilities and challenges of approaching and revisiting a story in different ways?

3. Considering the collection of children's literature and different book types in my classroom collection or library, which stories lend themselves to multiple reads? For a particular book, which kind of read would I plan to do first? Second? Third? Notice how this order might vary depending on the content of the book and your purposes for reading and discussing it.

Chapter 6
Idea Investigations: Extending the Read-Aloud Experience

**Students thrive when they have opportunities
to continue delving into their questions and ideas!**
—Ashley Wishart, Classroom Teacher

"If I were to cut the cake, I would have divided it waaaaaay differently."

"How they cut it . . . That just wasn't fair!"

"Yeah, the elephant is big, but so is the lion and it was *his* birthday!"

As Ms. Burris's third-grade students enter the classroom the next day, they continue debating ideas of fair and equal. She overhears these comments from students as they are hanging up their coats and backpacks. Ms. Burris is excited to hear students continuing to think about *The Lion's Share* (McElligott 2012) and hone their arguments for and against the animals' actions. Since the Math Lens read-aloud the previous day, she too has continued to think about how the cake was cut, if it was fair, and her students' ideas about fractions. The story and the characters seeded new ideas and questions about portions and how fair and equal are similar and different. Students remain invested in thinking about portions, fair, and equal *within* the context of the lion's birthday party and the cake. Listening to students' comments as they settle into their morning routine, she jots a note about what she hears. She is excited to plan an Idea Investigation that will allow the class to extend this powerful thinking and weave together students' ideas from the Story Explore and Math Lens read-alouds.

Experiences beyond the read-aloud, what we call *Idea Investigations*, provide continued and plentiful learning opportunities after the read-aloud is finished. Once a classroom community has come to know a story context deeply through an Open Notice and Wonder read, and has thought together within that context as readers and mathematicians through Story Explore and Math Lens reads, we find Idea Investigations to be a meaningful way to continue thinking about students' questions and ideas. We find that students often become increasingly immersed in the story and begin to make meaningful connections to their own lives. As a result, we can ask deeper questions, and the learning extends beyond the pages of the book into a child's world. Our aim is to extend students' thinking through investigations that are responsive to, and inspired by, what emerges from the read-alouds and discussions. The concept of Idea Investigations is thoughtful and complex and is a bold contrast to typical extension activities such as worksheets or individual seatwork that take just a few moments, and little thinking, to complete.

Let's rejoin Ms. Hadreas and her first-grade students to see where they go next with *Last Stop on Market Street* (de la Peña 2015). We'll drop in as they engage in two Idea Investigations, one investigation that extends students' thinking about CJ's feelings that were the focus of the Story Explore read as well as a second investigation about the sense of community highlighted by the Math Lens read. After that, we'll also revisit Ms. Burris's class to hear where students go with ideas about fair and equal through an investigation that integrates students' ideas from the Story Explore and Math Lens reads of *The Lion's Share*.

Story Explore Idea Investigation in Action: Ms. Hadreas's Primary Classroom Continues with *Last Stop on Market Street*

In the Story Explore read-aloud of *Last Stop on Market Street*, Ms. Hadreas and her students focused on the range of emotions CJ experienced across the story, and by the end of the read-aloud students generated a long list of feeling words. Ms. Hadreas couldn't help but notice how engaged her students were in thinking about and discussing CJ's feelings. She decided to provide an Idea Investigation so that her students could continue their thinking and make connections between the story and their own lives. (See Figure 6.1.) Please see Appendix D for a copy of this planning template.

IDEA INVESTIGATION
Book Title and Author: Last Stop on Market Street written by Matt de la Peña, illustrated by Christian Robinson
Idea Investigation (Discussing, Drawing, Writing) What interactive experience will extend the mathematical and/or literary thinking? Continued focus on feelings. Make connections between charted feelings and feelings students have experienced in their own lives.
Which read-aloud discussion(s) does this investigation extend? ○ Math Lens ◉ Story Explore ○ Integrated Math Lens and Story Explore How does the investigation build on and deepen children's ideas about the math and/or literacy in the story and our discussions of the story? Encourage students to think about feelings and make connections to their own lives. Making connections is a powerful way to deepen understanding of themes and ideas in stories.

How will I launch the investigation?

- Review the charted list of feelings. Ask:
  Have you experienced one of these feelings in your own life? What happened?
  What was that like? Who was there with you?
- Choose one of the feelings from our chart.
- Write the feeling at the top of a blank piece of paper.
- Draw to describe/explore the feeling.
- Write at least one sentence describing the experience.

Materials
What materials do we need?
- Blank paper
- Crayons
- Pencils

Sharing Out Thinking, Ideas, and Work

When and how will students share their work?
◉ As they work
○ After they work
○ Whole group
◉ Small groups

What will I listen to/for or notice about students' work?
- Accurate description of feelings event (use of feelings–related vocabulary)
- Clear description of event and context (clarity of written and drawn ideas)

Figure 6.1
Ms. Hadreas's Planning Template for a Story Explore Idea Investigation with
Last Stop on Market Street

Ms. Hadreas: We looked at CJ's feelings across the story. They changed. Let's look at the ways (*gestures to the feelings chart*) they changed. We saw he was sad, disappointed, surprised, angry, and upset. But then Nana helped him notice the rainbow, and we noticed he was calm, excited, helpful, and glad! I would like for you to think about a time when you had one of these feelings or perhaps another feeling. Close your eyes like CJ and think about what was happening and maybe who was there with you. Can you picture who was there and what was happening?

Sulamite: I felt sad because . . . *(pausing as she continues thinking)*.

Dylan: I felt annoyed because I wanted a toy robot, but my parents wouldn't buy me one. They said it was too expensive.

Reem: I was happy because my dad took me to the park to play on the playground and go down the slide.

Sulamite: *(Continuing after gathering her thoughts)* I felt sad because my mom misses her sister, but she lives far away and I can't do anything to help bring her to this country.

Ms. Hadreas: These are all such good ideas and connections. I want everyone to spend some time thinking about the powerful feelings we've captured on this chart. Here's what we are going to do. We'll give everyone a piece of paper and you're going to picture yourself feeling one of these feelings. Write the word for this feeling at the top of the page and draw a picture to go with it. Draw yourself, what your face looked like, how you felt, and what was happening. Write at least one sentence about your experience with this feeling at the bottom of the page.

Ms. Hadreas chose this Idea Investigation to encourage students to think deeply about the feelings in the story and also to make connections to their own lives. The investigation, while needing a bit of thinking and planning, did not require complicated materials. She invites students to use blank paper, crayons, and pencils, all readily available in the classroom. This simplicity of materials allows her to prepare for the investigation quickly and to focus her thoughts more on ideas and less on materials.

Ms. Hadreas also had several other Idea Investigations in mind, in addition to the feelings drawing, that she could have had her students explore instead. One was to utilize a simple two-circle Venn diagram handout, prompting students to think about a time they went with an adult in their family somewhere for the day, comparing and contrasting their experience to CJ and Nana's journey. She also thought of focusing on the sequence of events in the story, using a five-box storyboard handout to encourage students to explore a similar sequence of events in their own lives. For this Idea Investigation, she would prompt students to think of, describe, and illustrate a trip taken with an adult family member, using the storyboard to sequence their story using words and illustrations. She would have prompted students with who, what, when, where, why, and how questions to help them develop their sequence:

- Who were you going with?
- What did you see along the way?
- When did you go?
- Where did you go?
- Why were you going there?
- How did you get there?

Although both of these additional ideas would have made thoughtful and engaging extension experiences, Ms. Hadreas decided to stick with the idea of exploring feelings and making connections to students' lives, based primarily on their interest and enthusiasm, something that she hopes will result in deeper understanding of CJ's character and the sequence of story events.

Planning for Idea Investigations in Your Classroom

Our goal in planning for an Idea Investigation is to carefully consider students' ideas that emerged during previous reads and think about how to deepen and extend those ideas in a meaningful way. Sometimes the ideas for an investigation present themselves through the process of multiple reads. Other times, we must step back from the charted ideas and students' work to consider what a thoughtful mathematical and/or literary investigation might be.

The Idea Investigations Planning Template (Figure 6.2) walks you through questions to aid in your investigation design. You'll begin by thinking about how to extend, build on, and deepen students' thinking. If possible, we want to create a through line by carrying forward themes in students' ideas from Open Notice and Wonder, Story Explore, and Math Lens reads.

We ask, does this Idea Investigation grow from a Story Explore read (as we saw with Ms. Hadreas and the investigation of students' feelings after focusing on CJ's feelings during the Story Explore read)? Does it grow from a Math Lens read? Or does it integrate students' ideas from the Story Explore and the Math Lens reads? Next, you'll jot ideas about how to launch the investigation with students. After sketching in this portion of the planning template, you may want to transfer your ideas to sticky notes and place them *on* the book

IDEA INVESTIGATION

Book Title and Author

Idea Investigation (Discussing, Drawing, Writing)
What interactive experience will extend the mathematical and/or literary thinking?

Which read-aloud discussion(s) does this investigation extend?
○ Math Lens
○ Story Explore
○ Integrated Math Lens and Story Explore

How does the investigation build on and deepen children's ideas about the math and/or literacy in the story and our discussions of the story?

How will I launch the investigation?

Materials
What materials do we need?

Sharing Out Thinking, Ideas, and Work

When and how will students share their work?
○ As they work
○ After they work
○ Whole group
○ Small groups

What will I listen to/for or notice about students' work?

Figure 6.2
Idea Investigation Planning Template
(For a reproducible copy of this template, see Appendix D.)

or have your planning template handy to refer to during the launch. The planning template also includes a prompt to help you consider what materials to gather. After that, we find it helpful to consider how students will work and when they will share their ideas. Will they work in small groups or as a whole group? If working in small groups, when and how will students share their ideas? Will they share their thinking-in-progress with the others through a pause and check-in as they work to spur each other's thinking? Or will they share their thinking after fleshing out their ideas and creating an artifact for a whole-group strategy share? Finally, we can plan ahead to guide what we will listen for and why. As students work and share their ideas, it is an ideal time for us to listen to their sense making. We can hear what students understand and what they are coming to understand.

We use these overarching ideas to guide our thinking and planning for powerful Idea Investigations:

Powerful Idea Investigations

- Have a through line from Open Notice and Wonder, Story Explore, Math Lens reads

- Continue to focus on students' ideas

- Work to deepen understanding of the mathematics and/or comprehension of the story and related elements

- Make connections to students' lived experiences and invite children to draw on their cultural ways of knowing and being

- Are open-ended, complex tasks with many possible solutions and viewpoints; have broad access among students

- Open up opportunities for creative expression and productive struggle

- Use simple materials

Idea Investigations Are Not

- Worksheets or activities with limited opportunities for complex thinking

- Constrained activities prompting funneled responses or solutions

- Rote tasks focused on arithmetic or decoding words

Planning time is best spent *thinking* about a powerful experience for students and gathering simple tools to support their Idea Investigation. We encourage teachers to use simple materials such as pencils, crayons, and blank paper, for several reasons:

1. Planning moments are best spent focused on the story and the ideas and questions students generate.

2. Material costs are kept down by avoiding using resources to print or copy worksheets.

3. Flexibility is maximized, as students can use simple tools and materials during investigations in the classroom or in remote-learning settings.

4. Creative thinking is emphasized, as blank paper encourages students to use their creativity and sense of artistic design—layout, organization, scale, color, and spacing.

Math Lens Idea Investigation in Action: Ms. Hadreas's First-Grade Classroom Continues with *The Last Stop on Market Street*

Ms. Hadreas feels inspired by the way her students were thinking about this story. The evolution of their ideas from the Open Notice and Wonder, into the Story Explore and Math Lens reads, to the literacy-focused Idea Investigation had been a collective journey over the week. As she stands over her desk, holding and studying the students' feeling drawings from the Story Explore Idea Investigation, Ms. Hadreas sees that these students drew images of a wide variety of feelings, across a range of life experiences, with many different people in their lives (Figures 6.3 and 6.4). An idea for an additional investigation begins to formulate in Ms. Hadreas's mind, and she sits down with the book and an Idea Investigation planning template to sketch her thinking (Figure 6.5). She wants to challenge students to think about (and grapple with) the multiple communities of which they are a part and the magnitude of community and to come to see that they shape and are shaped by the people in their world.

Figure 6.3
A Student's Drawing of "Sad" from the Story Explore
Idea Investigation of *Last Stop on Market Street*

Figure 6.4
A Student's Drawing of "Happe" and "angre"
from the Story Explore Idea Investigation of
Last Stop on Market Street

IDEA INVESTIGATION

Book Title and Author: Last Stop on Market Street written by Matt de la Peña, illustrated by Christian Robinson

Idea Investigation (Discussing, Drawing, Writing)
What interactive experience will extend the mathematical and/or literary thinking?

As a whole group, brainstorm different communities in students' lives. Invite students to select one community they are a part of, think about how many people are in that community, and describe how they help and are helped by their community.

Which read-aloud discussion(s) does this investigation extend?

◉ Math Lens
○ Story Explore
○ Integrated Math Lens and Story Explore

How does the investigation build on and deepen children's ideas about the math and/or literacy in the story and our discussions of the story?

Continued focus on the magnitude of community, how a community shapes us, and looking from the story to communities in students' own lives.

How will I launch the investigation?

- Picture walk through CJ's communities in the book.
- Discuss that we are all part of multiple communities.
- Brainstorm different types of community, define community using students' ideas and words.
- Invite students to focus on one community they are a part of.

Materials
What materials do we need?
- Blank paper
- Crayons and markers
- Pencils
- Counting tools (ten-frames, Unifix cubes)

Sharing Out Thinking, Ideas, and Work

When and how will students share their work?

- ⦿ As they work
- ○ After they work
- ⦿ Whole group
- ○ Small groups

What will I listen to/for or notice about students' work?

- How are students counting and recording the people in their community?
- How are students thinking and talking about quantity?
- How are students using the story context to think about themselves as a part of a community?

Figure 6.5
Ms. Hadreas's Planning Template for a Math Lens Idea Investigation with *Last Stop on Market Street*

Ms. Hadreas: This story *(holding up the book)* has become a special part of our classroom! We have begun to feel that CJ, Nana, and their community are people we know, like his friends on the bus *(showing an illustration on the bus)* and people in the soup kitchen *(holding up that page)*. You counted the number of people, using tally marks and ten-frames and counting by ones and tens. We had a lively discussion, and we could see there are many people in CJ's community. We can also see that CJ is a part of several different communities *(thumbing through and displaying the pages)*. He is a part of a community at his church, on the bus, and at the soup kitchen. Like CJ, you are a part of many different communities. Take a moment to think, what different communities are you a part of? When you have ideas, turn and share with, and listen to, your neighbor.

After a few moments of think time, students start sharing their ideas. Ms. Hadreas overhears:

"I am a part of my family."

"I'm on a soccer team."

"We are all in this class."

"I go to church like CJ."

"My neighborhood."

"Our family goes to the park a lot, is that a community?"

She decides to bring the group back together and brainstorm, share, and record their multiple communities. She begins writing the ideas she overhears on chart paper.

Ms. Hadreas: I was listening to you share the communities you are a part of in your life. I began recording your ideas here *(pointing to the chart)*. What can we add on to this list?

Khaled:	Is a park a community?

Ms. Hadreas:	*(Turning to the group)* I hear us wanting to be clearer about what we mean by community. What are your thoughts? Is a park a community? What is a community?

The students continue to generate and refine their working definition of community. They decide a community is a group of people who spend time together in the same place or who like to do the same things. They think communities help each other and play or solve problems together and that there is a "belonging feeling" of being in a community. With this definition in mind, they brainstorm their collective list of communities, adding the library, clay studio, community center, friends, our town, museum, neighborhood grocery store, baseball team, Wushu Martial Arts Club, chess club, music lessons, YMCA Boys and Girls Club, and extended family including cousins and grandparents.

Ms. Hadreas:	Each of us is a part of *many* communities. I'd like for you to think about a community that is important to you. Then, using this blank piece of paper, draw yourself in that community. You can draw other people and any activities you do together in your community. I want you to think about how many people are a part of that community. Count the people, if you can, or estimate, and write a number to show how many people are in your community. Last, I want you to think about your role in your community. How do you give help? How do you receive help? I've put these questions on chart paper for us to look at while we work. I'll come around to listen to your ideas and ask questions to help you think.

As students spread out across the room, drawing, counting, writing numbers and equations, and sharing their ideas with classmates around them, Ms. Hadreas kneels down next to children. She asks them questions, such as:

- "Can you tell me about your community?"

- "Can I listen to you count the people in your community?"

- "How are you keeping track of the people?"

- "What does it look like to write the number 16?"

Ms. Hadreas listens to hear if the task is open-ended enough—does it allow for multiple and varied creative responses from children? Is there broad access? Are all children finding a way into the task? She believes so, as she listens in.

The next day, after students had created their community drawings, counted a quantity for their community, and considered ideas about how they help and are helped by their community, the class engages in a whole-group discussion. Ms. Hadreas chose to wait to have the discussion the next day so that students might talk with their families and perhaps gain a fuller idea of how many people were in their selected community and what their roles as community members might be. Gathered together on the carpet, students begin to share about their communities.

As students excitedly name their communities out loud, Ms. Hadreas sketches a visual on chart paper (Figure 6.6). While she sketches, she narrates what she hears, "Mako, I hear you saying you are a part of our classroom community, your family, and the Wushu Martial Arts Center. Let me see if I can create some overlap in the bubbles to show that you're a part of multiple communities!" As more children share their overlapping communities, she realizes this is a complicated idea to sketch! She does her best to show some of the overlap but turns her focus to capturing the many communities that students are a part of and clustering some of the nested communities, such as a neighborhood, park, and community center. She also tries to create a bubble that reflects a typical size of such a community.

Interesting noticings about the size of a community's space and the typical number of people in those spaces emerge. For example, "A library is big and a lot of people could fit inside but sometimes there are many people and sometimes there is just some" and "The park is really big! On Saturday there is lots of families but one time at night we were the only family!" As Ms. Hadreas listens and continues sketching, students begin to see that they are a part of many different communities and that communities can be made up of a few people or lots and lots of people, with students making comments like, "Wow! We are in so many communities!" and "Some communities are smaller, and some are really *big*!" (See Figure 6.6.)

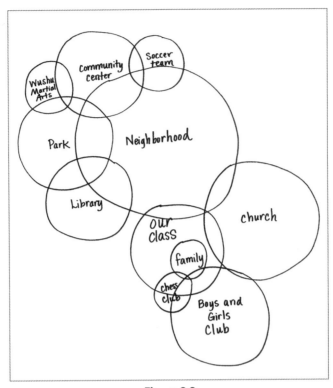

Figure 6.6
Ms. Hadreas's Class Communities Sketch

An emerging idea through the exploration Ms. Hadreas has with her students is that a community is important and can have big impact, no matter its size. As Ms. Hadreas listens, she feels energized and wants to continue to discuss students' ideas in the coming days—especially the idea that a student is an individual but also an important part of different communities and that each child has a responsibility to shape and be shaped by their communities. She wonders if ideas about students actualizing their agency to create new communities might emerge.

Integrated Math Lens and Story Explore Idea Investigation in Action: Ms. Burris's Third-Grade Classroom Continues with *The Lion's Share*

As Ms. Burris sits down to sketch her ideas on a planning template, she makes sure to sit where she can view the charted ideas from both of the previous reads and discussions of the story.

The previous day Ms. Burris had jotted a note with the questions about how students would cut the cake and whether fair is the same as equal. As she thinks more, she decides to add a question about justification (Why would you cut the cake in that way?) and to orient students to the story context as they think more about their ideas (How did the story and the animals' behaviors influence your decision about how to cut the cake?). *When we mathematize stories, we want to be sure to continue to refer to, and delve into, the story context as a powerful resource for thinking mathematically.*

Hearing students' ideas as they come into the classroom in the morning gives Ms. Burris the perfect opportunity to launch an investigation (Figure 6.7).

IDEA INVESTIGATION

Book Title and Author: The Lion's Share written by Matthew McElligott

Idea Investigation (Discussing, Drawing, Writing)
What interactive experience will extend the mathematical and/or literary thinking?

Invite students to discuss and decide how they would divide the cake among the animals at Lion's dinner party and why.

Which read-aloud discussion(s) does this investigation extend?
○ Math Lens
○ Story Explore
◉ Integrated Math Lens and Story Explore

How does the investigation build on and deepen children's ideas about the math and/or literacy in the story and our discussions of the story?

- Continue our focus on the ideas of fair vs. equal and dividing the cake into portions using the story context.
- Discuss and justify how students choose to cut the cake and what fraction of the cake each animal should receive.
- Begin naming and labeling fractional amounts.

How will I launch the investigation?

Revisit how the animals in the story cut the cake and how it seemed problematic when considering "fair" and "equal." Post and share these questions:

- How would you cut the cake?
- Why are you cutting it in that way?
- How did the story and the characters influence your decision about how to cut the cake?
- Is fair the same as equal? Why?

Describe how students may get started—gather materials, share their ideas-in-progress, think together about the story and how to cut and why. Prepare to share and justify their plan for cutting the cake.

Materials

What materials do we need?

- Construction paper in different colors
- Graph paper
- Pencils and markers
- Rulers
- Scissors

Sharing Out Thinking, Ideas, and Work

When and how will students share their work?

○ As they work
◉ After they work
◉ Whole group
○ Small groups

What will I listen to/for or notice about students' work?

- How are students dividing the cake and crafting an argument in response to the four guiding questions?
- How are students thinking and talking about fair vs. equal and the relative sizes of the pieces?
- What fractional amounts are students curious about, and what fractions do they tend to understand and are they coming to understand?

Figure 6.7
Ms. Burris's Planning Template for an Integrated Idea Investigation with *The Lion's Share*

Ms. Burris: I can hear that you're continuing to think about how the animals cut the cake in *The Lion's Share*. I kept thinking about this last night, too! The way the animals chose to cut the cake . . . It really made us think! Today, I would like for us to continue this thinking, together. Specifically, I want you to reason about these questions *(pointing to the easel and reading the questions aloud)* (Figure 6.8). As you think through your ideas for how *you* would cut the cake and *why*, consider what happened in the story that influences your thinking. Use details in the story to strengthen your argument! On the side table are some tools to help you develop and represent your thinking. You'll find different colors of construction paper, graph paper, markers, rulers, pencils, and scissors. There are extra copies of the book, too, if you want to revisit the pages and study the animals and how they cut the cake. I'd like for us to work in small groups. You do not have to have your idea fully formed yet. You will continue to shape your argument through your discussion of the story and by hearing and considering each other's ideas. Practice supporting your argument with ideas or examples from the story and be ready to share your argument. We will be sharing our solutions and our justifications as a whole group.

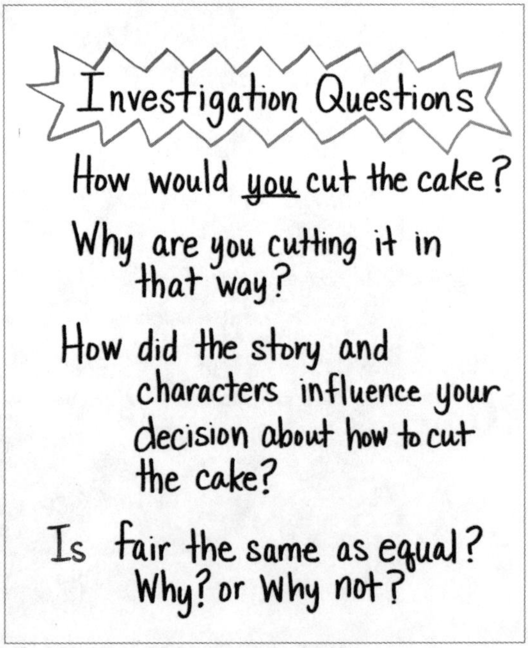

As students get settled at desks, at tables, and in different nooks around the room, Ms. Burris stands near the supply table to listen to students and support them to get underway in their work. She hears students deciding which tools will help their thinking and beginning to make conjectures as they get to work. She overhears:

"I'm thinking about the size of the animal. And I think how much cake

Figure 6.8
Investigation Questions for *The Lion's Share*

each animal should get should be based on its size. Like, maybe the elephant should get a half of the cake!?"

"I think the animal's behavior determines the size of cake it deserves. If you are greedy, you get a small piece. *But* the ant, even though she is small, gets a huge piece because she was *not* greedy."

Hearing different ideas, Ms. Burris senses a lively debate and discussion, which is just what she was hoping for! Moving around the room, she kneels beside students to listen and ask about their ideas. She often glances to the easel to remember the focal questions (Figure 6.8) and poses those questions as a way to enter into, or support, students' discussions.

As she listens to students' reasoning, Ms. Burris notices that all groups are imagining their cake to be rectangular like the cake in the story. She also notices distinctions emerging as she hears three big ideas developing across the groups. One is the idea that the cake should be cut into ten equal pieces so that every animal gets the same portion. The groups who settle on this solution argue that it is fair and it is equal. Despite the animals' differing behaviors and sizes, it is best to have all the pieces of cake be the same size. Ms. Burris observes that one group using this solution cuts the cake (a green piece of construction paper) into ten vertical slices, almost like long columns and labels each slice as ⅒ (Figure 6.9). Another group draws one line across the page of blue construction paper horizontally, creating two rows each divided into five columns. They cut ten rectangles of cake (Figure 6.10).

A second common idea among the class is that the portion of cake should match the size of the animal. "Biggest animals get the biggest portion, smallest animals get the smallest portions!" As Ms. Burris listens to

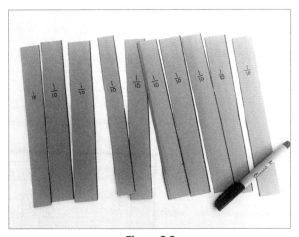

Figure 6.9
Ten Vertical Slices of Cake

Figure 6.10
Ten Rectangles of Cake

these students' reasoning, she hears them working to determine the relative size of each animal:

"Elephant must be biggest!"

"Is a gorilla bigger than a lion or a lion bigger than a gorilla?"

"That depends! What does it look like with the gorilla and lion in our story?"

"A beetle is smaller than a frog but bigger than an ant!"

Once students agree on the order of size of the animals in the story, they turn their attention to the fractional amounts of cake necessary for this solution. One group settles upon the idea that Lion and Elephant are biggest and therefore should each receive a half of a half or one-fourth of the whole cake. They sketch their thinking on chart paper (Figure 6.11). Next, they decide that the rest of the animals, since "they are kind of smaller" will share the remaining portion of cake. They discuss how to divide up the remaining half among eight animals.

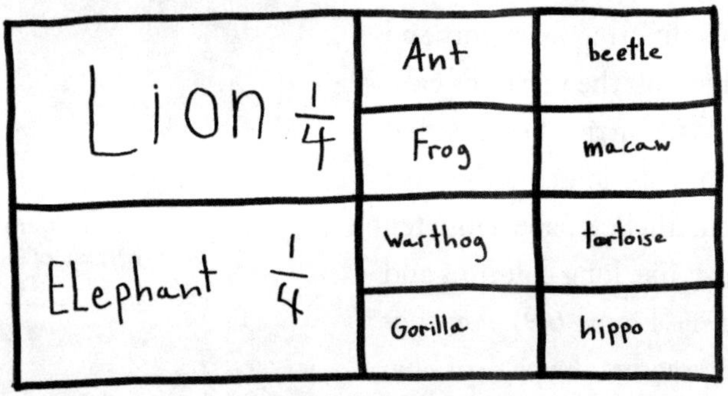

Figure 6.11
Students' Sketch for Biggest Animal, Biggest Portion

Students wonder what portion of the whole cake the rest of the animals will each get and how to name and label each portion:

"The rest of the animals—there are eight of them—will share the other half of the cake."

"So we need to divide one-half of the cake into eight equal parts."

"We could carry the line across *(pointing to the half line dividing Lion and Elephant's portions)* and that would divide the remaining part in half."

"Let's draw across and up and down *(gesturing horizontal and vertical lines)* to divide each fourth into fourths."

"So what is this portion *(pointing to one of the other animal's smaller portions)*? What is that?!

"Is it one eighth? Because it is a fourth of a half?"

"No! It is a fourth of a fourth! Because we have to look at the whole cake."

"Let's see if we can figure this out. This is really stretching my brain!"

A different group that is also pursuing the biggest animal, biggest portion solution decides that each animal should receive a different portion on a sliding scale of size (Figure 6.12). Lion and Elephant each receive one-fourth of the whole cake, Gorilla and Hippo each get a half of a fourth of the cake, Warthog gets less than Gorilla and Hippo but more than Tortoise, while Tortoise, Macaw, and Frog all get the same amount, and finally Ant and Beetle share the last bit. These students question and reason as they divide out the portions:

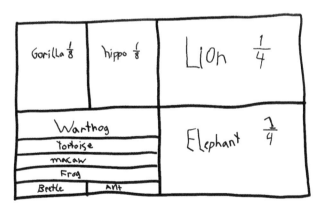

Figure 6.12
Another Group's Sketch for Biggest Animal, Biggest Portion

"Tortoise, Macaw, and Frog should be in one size group."

"And Warthog, it's a bit bigger than those but it is not as big as Gorilla and Hippo."

"Beetle and Ant are really small."

"So Lion and Elephant get one fourth, that is easy."

"Then a half of a fourth is an eighth of the cake."

"I start to get unsure with Warthog's piece."

"I do too."

"Let's label what we can like one-fourth and then one-eighth."

"What is a third of a fourth? That's what I think Warthog has but I don't know how to say it in a fraction! It is like, one two out of six of a fourth."

"Whoa!"

"I think this plan *is* fair but I do *not* think it is equal."

"The size of the pieces *is* equal for some animals, like Beetle and Ant are getting the same amount as each other but it is *not* equal across the animals."

Ms. Burris is excited to hear students asking questions about portions and grappling with complex mathematical ideas. She can hear their emerging ideas about portions that are supported by the story and are more nuanced than their typical math discussions. She can hear opportunities to engage in sense making about portions smaller than what they would tend to study, such as a third of a fourth or two-sixths (or one-third) of a fourth. She comments to the whole group, "I notice you're experimenting with new fractions. Exciting! Some people are starting to show their thinking by labeling their cake portions. You're welcome to experiment with labeling your pieces, if you would like to."

A third big idea students have is cutting the cake according to the animals' behavior:

"If you are greedy, you get a small piece. If you are generous, polite, or kind, you get a large piece." The students using this strategy are deeply engaged in democratic debate, within the story context, and are passionate about the pieces not being equal. They follow a less systematic cutting strategy, of measuring and drawing, to make extreme differences in the size of the portion—beginning with cutting tiny slices off of each corner and then dividing the rest down the middle.

> "The lion gets the biggest portion because he waited patiently, and it was *his* party!"

> "The ant gets the next biggest because she also waited."

> "All the other animals get a teeny tiny piece because they were *so greedy*!"

> "How can we show that?"

> "Let's cut tiny tiny pieces and then the big rest of the cake is half for the lion and half for the ant!"

> "Yes! Let's take a few miniscule pieces from this corner *(pointing to the construction paper)* and a few miniscule pieces from the other corner."

> "Smaller than miniscule—crumbs!!"

> "How much is a crumb? Like one-one hundredth?"

> "Yeah, like one-one hundredth of the cake!"

> "This is *all* you get *(pointing to the tiny cut out pieces)*!" (See Figure 6.13.)

Figure 6.13
"This is *all* you get!"

Ms. Burris carries a clipboard with paper, as she listens to students at work. She jots down students' strategies to help her pay attention to the details of their thinking and to think about how to select and sequence their solutions in the whole-group discussion (Smith and Stein 2011). She sketches a table to organize her notes (Figure 6.14). She listens for a range of strategies and notes which ideas are emerging so she can elicit a broad range of solutions and justifications—that are grounded in the story context—in the discussion. She listens not only for *which* ideas are emerging, but also *who* is the author of those ideas so she can intentionally include a broad range of voices in the discussion. By listening carefully to children whose voices she is working to expand in the classroom community, she can help make sure that students who tend to participate as active listeners also have their ideas heard and considered.

Strategy	Students' Thinking	Students	Order for Sharing
Portion of cake is tied to animal's behavior	"Greediest animals get smallest portions." "It is not equal but it's fair."	Elliot, Luis, and Peder Leo and Naomi	Third
Every animal gets the same size portion	"Every piece is equal size." "This is the most fair."	Neeku and Roshann Aram and Grace	First
Biggest animal gets biggest portion	"Size depends on size of the animal." "It is fair for how much each animal can eat but it's not equal."	Julia, Maya, and Anika Ayana and Adisa	Second

Figure 6.14
Ms. Burris's Notes While Listening to Children Investigate
The Lion's Share. **(For a reproducible copy of this note-taking form, see Appendix E.)**

Using her sketched notes, Ms. Burris plans for and facilitates a discussion that allows the three main strategies to emerge. She opens the conversation by inviting Neeku and Roshann, students who cut all the pieces the same size, to share first. Next, Ayana and Adisa describe their ideas about the biggest animals getting the biggest portions. Finally, Leo and Naomi argue for why they believe the portion must be connected to the animals' behavior. Throughout the discussion, she reiterates the focal questions for this Idea Investigation. As each group shares their thinking, she asks, "How are you choosing to cut the cake?" and "Why are you cutting it in that way?" and "How did the story and the characters influence your decision about how to cut the cake?" Students, listening to their classmates' thinking, often ask, "Do you think your strategy is fair? Do you think your strategy is equal? Why?" The discussion is lively and supports young mathematicians to do the following:

- Engage in emerging thinking about portions and the many different ways a whole can be divided.

- Use the story context to develop, explain, and justify their ideas.

- Ask new questions about mathematics because of the story context.

- Engage in productive struggle and persevere in thinking about complex mathematics.

- Develop more robust norms around justification and argumentation as a mathematical community.

- Elevate the voices of community members and expand students' views of themselves and of each other as mathematicians.

Additional Idea Investigation Suggestions and Examples

Through our work with teachers and students, we have facilitated, observed, and listened to many inspiring discussions that extend a read-aloud experience in meaningful ways. We will briefly describe some of these Idea Investigation suggestions and examples and hope they inspire your own innovation with investigations!

This Is a Ball (Stanton and Stanton 2017)

When we think about mathematical opportunities within children's literature, we often think about mathematical content. We ask ourselves, "What are the mathematical ideas that children could think about within this story context?" We have come to discover that there are also vibrant opportunities to think about, and engage in, discussion of mathematical practices through stories. Such practices include making sense of problems and persevering in solving them; arguing; modeling; or making use of structure (Common Core State Standards for Mathematical Practice 2011). In the case of the book *This Is a Ball*, the practice of argumentation—or constructing viable arguments—takes center stage!

We learned about this story from Erin Gannon and Kristin Gray, who at the time were a literacy coach and a math coach working together at an elementary school. Within the pages of the story, the author makes outrageous claims that provoke laughter and spur playful disagreement. This text-dependent story and its intriguing illustrations push young mathematicians to articulate their position and provide evidence for their reasoning. For example, as Ms. Gannon shows children the cover, young mathematicians erupt in argumentation with the book! "That is *not* a ball! That is a

cube!" Or when she turns to a page that shows a simple drawing of a car, declaring, "This is a bike," children shout back, "Noooooo! That is a car!" The text continues, "Look at the wheels. It's definitely a bike." Causing children to insist, "That car has four wheels. A bike has two wheels and you sit on it, not *in* it!" Through each example, young mathematicians not only express their disagreement, they are compelled to describe details of *why* they disagree.

We also notice the power of collective argumentation among children and against the book. Although disagreement of ideas happens often in mathematical discussions and is some of our most exciting work, the disagreement tends to be about the ideas and between mathematicians in the classroom community. In the case of this book, there is collective power and *joy* in arguing together against the story itself!

After sharing the story, Ms. Gannon designs an investigation to continue students' reasoning and argumentation. For kindergarteners, she creates a ten-frame with four dots and writes "This is a 5" (Figure 6.15). She displays the image and gives children a sheet with the image, and they set to work inspired by the story and their continued spirited outrage. For first-grade students, Ms. Gannon writes the equation 10 – 4 and the statement "This is 5." Similarly, children argue for whether they agree or disagree with the statement and *why* (Figures 6.16, 6.17, 6.18). The argumentation and reasoning that ensues for both groups is lively, engaging, and complex, both orally and, for the first graders, in writing.

This is 5.

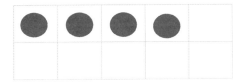

Figure 6.15
"This Is 5" Ten-Frame Image

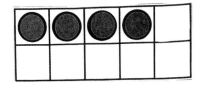

Figure 6.16
"This Is 5" Student Response. (*No, that is for. If you think 2 + 2 = 5. You are rog!*)

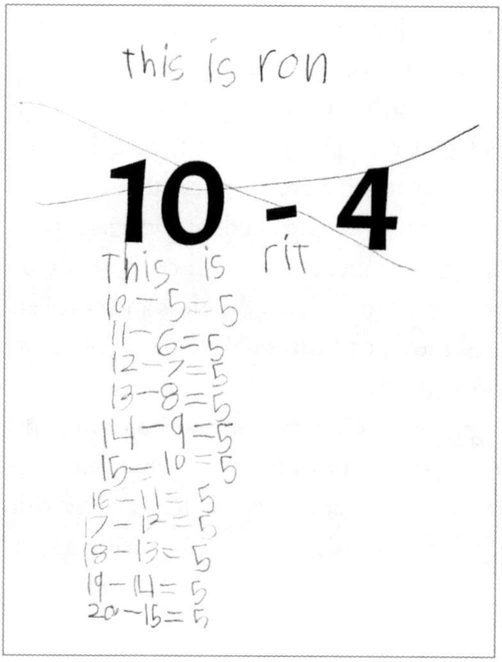

Figure 6.17
"This Is 5" Student Response (*This is ron. This is rit*)

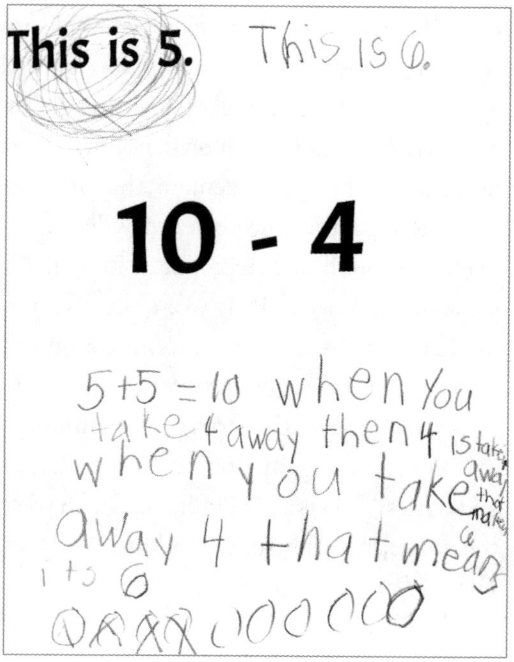

Figure 6.18
"This Is 5" Student Response (*This is 6*)

Full House: An Invitation to Fractions (Dodds 2009)

You'll remember briefly reading about this story in Chapter 3 as we described text-dependent book types. In this playful story, characters visit the Strawberry Inn, which has six rooms, one of which is where the innkeeper, Miss Bloom, lives. As the guests arrive and settle into their rooms, one by one, one-sixth of the inn is filled. There is a fraction notation at the bottom of the page to show how many rooms are full. For example, when the first guest arrives and checks into room number one, the story reads, "One room of six had a guest for the night" and the fraction $\frac{1}{6}$ is shown. When the second guest arrives, "two rooms of six" have guests and $\frac{2}{6}$ is shown. This pattern continues until all five of the guests have checked in and the inn is full because Miss Bloom lives in one of the six rooms.

As Mr. Llorente and his third-grade students read and discuss this story, a thrilling debate erupts about whether the Inn is full at $\frac{5}{6}$ or $\frac{6}{6}$. Here is short portion of their discussion:

Iris: I think the inn will be full at $\frac{5}{6}$ because then all the guest rooms will be full and so the inn will be full.

Mr. Llorente: Can someone add on to what Iris is thinking?

Rowan:	I hadn't thought about it that way. What Iris is saying is that when there are five people at the inn *all* the rooms for guests will be full. So, she said that the inn will be full when it is $\frac{5}{5}$.
Dieder:	I disagree because $\frac{5}{6}$ is not full, $\frac{5}{6}$ is not a whole, it would be $\frac{6}{6}$ when it is full.
Mr. Llorente:	Let's get some more ideas out on the table.
Nayah:	I agree with Iris's idea because there are five rooms for the guests and once those rooms are full there are no more rooms for people to stay in.
Dieder:	Who is right? Is Iris right?
Mr. Llorente:	It is not about being right, it is about making sense of what is happening in this book and using the story and illustrations to think about your ideas. Turn and talk with someone by you. What do you think and *why* do you think that?

As Mr. Llorente listens in, he can hear disagreement in the students' reasoning. Throughout the spirited discussion, students add on to and think within others' ideas, and a student even stands up to exclaim, "What you just said makes *so much sense!*"

For the Idea Investigation, Mr. Llortente lays out blank paper, pencils, markers, rulers, clipboards, and photocopies of the page from the story showing the inn. He asks students to create a drawing that will help them argue for $\frac{5}{5}$ or $\frac{6}{6}$ and write a justification. He wants to pursue the ideas students are raising that grow from, and beyond, the storyline in the book. He lets students know they will use their work to engage in a whole-class discussion the next day.

Over time, sharing and discussing their drawings, students collectively generate the idea that you have to think of the inn as $\frac{5}{5}$ + $\frac{1}{6}$. $\frac{5}{5}$ is full for guests—a No Vacancy sign would go up—and there is $\frac{1}{6}$ of the inn left, which is Miss Bloom's room. They ask, "So if $\frac{5}{6}$ + $\frac{1}{6}$ = $\frac{6}{6}$, could we also claim then that $\frac{6}{7}$ + $\frac{1}{7}$ = $\frac{7}{7}$ or $\frac{7}{8}$ + $\frac{1}{8}$ = $\frac{8}{8}$?" "It has to be but how could we prove it?" Mr. Llorente listens, believing it is important to discuss students' ideas as they grapple with defining the whole and how a whole can change. Dieder announces, "We have work to do!"

Splash! (Jonas 1997)

In a kindergarten classroom, after having enjoyed this text-dependent story several times and discussed the mathematics on various pages, Ms. Mortenson decides to have her students engage in an investigation involving creative play and movement. The gathering rug, at the center of their classroom, becomes an imaginary pond. Each child takes on the role of an animal from the charted list of the different animals in the story. Mia becomes a goldfish! Ali, a frog! Idris is the turtle, and Kala, the cat! As children take on their role, they pretend to move like their assigned animal. With everyone seated around the edge of the "pond," Ms. Mortenson reads through the book again page by page, and as she does, the children reenact story events by playing their various animal roles, jumping into or out of the pond to match what is happening in the book and its illustrations. "The turtle jumps into the pond," Ms. Mortensen reads, and plop, Idris jumps into the center of the rug. By the end of the story, almost everyone has a chance to jump into or out of the pond—except for a few!

Jose: I didn't get a turn!

Ms. Mortenson: What animal was your role?

Jose: A goldfish!

Ms. Mortenson: I see! I wonder, readers, why might Jose not have gotten a turn to jump out of the pond?

Several students: Because if a fish jumps out of the water it will *die*!

Jose: Oh yeah! That would be very bad!

One Is a Snail, Ten Is a Crab (Sayre and Sayre 2006)

Figure 6.19
One Is a Snail, Ten Is a Crab Illustration

In this story, readers are invited to count by number of feet as they view colorful illustrations of insects, snails, crabs, and a variety of other animals. One is a snail, two is a person, four is a dog, and ten is a crab! Mrs. Zimmerman and her third-grade students read this story several times and use the ideas and illustrations to open up different mathematical opportunities.

After students explore combinations of animal legs in the story and generate equations (as you read about in Chapter 5 with the example of planning for a Math Lens read that focuses on multiplication), Ms. Zimmerman narrows upon a particular illustration showing four crabs on the left-hand page and ten dogs on the right-hand page (Figure 6.19). She has made a color copy of this spread for each table group of children. Handing out the image to each small group of students, she displays the image under the document camera. Alongside the image is a chart paper with the question, "True or false?" above the equation $4 \times 10 = 10 \times 4$. Each student's job is to argue whether the statement is true or false and use the illustration to justify their claim to their group. Using the illustration as a support, students develop their claims. Arya, working alongside her classmate Jasmine, is heard counting the animals' feet:

Arya: *(Pointing to the four crabs)* On this page, there are 10, 20, 30, 40 legs on the crabs. *(Pointing to each crab as she counts by 10 and jots a 40 on her page)* And on this page *(moving over to the illustration with dogs, she points to the dog legs one by one),* hmm, it looks like there are more legs! There's 1, 2, 3, 4 legs on each dog. And there are 1, 2, 3 . . . 10 dogs. So that is . . . 4 legs on 10 dogs or 40 legs all together.

Jasmine: It's the same amount of legs!

Arya: Yes! Forty is the same as forty!

Students around the room discuss and work to prove, with agreement, that this equation is true. Relying on the illustration, they hone, justify, and prove their claim that four groups of ten is the same as ten groups of four. Students begin turning to other pages in the story to generate their own "True or False?" equations.

Dog's Colorful Day (Dodd 2003)

You may remember reading briefly about this story in Chapter 3 as an example of a text-dependent book; it was also mentioned in Chapter 5 as a potential book for a Story Explore read. *Dog's Colorful Day* combines counting one to ten with an adorable dog, an entertaining sequence of spots gathered by the dog, and a surprise at the end (Figures 6.20). After enjoying several reads of this story, Mr. Collins's first-grade students sit at tables with blank paper and colored pencils designing their own dog's colorful day journey and equations. Mr. Collins listens in and hears different students talking as they draw:

> "My dog has ten spots all different colors. A red spot is from stepping in a bucket of freshly picked strawberries."

> "My dog has six spots from a person with a Crayola!"

> "My dog has five spots because *I am five!*"

Figure 6.20
Dog's Colorful Day Illustration

As students decide how many spots and what the spots are from, Mr. Collins invites them to add numbers or equations and/or descriptive sentences to their drawings. Students write numbers and some begin to add an addition equation. He overhears how students are beginning to see spots in groups and express that with addition (Figures 6.21, 6.22, 6.23, and 6.24.)

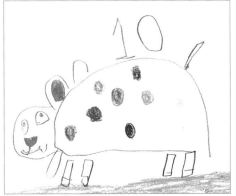

Figure 6.21
Student Drawing with One Red Spot from Freshly Picked Strawberries

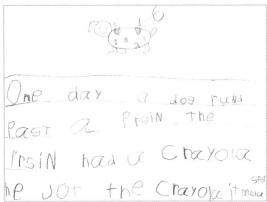

Figure 6.22
Student Work with Six Spots from a "Prsin" with a Crayola

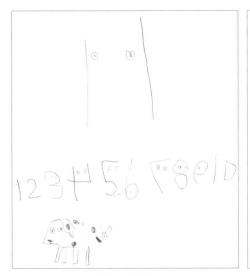

Figure 6.23
Student Work with Two Yellow Spots from a Lemonade Stand

Figure 6.24
Student Work with Five Spots

For example, one student says, "My dog has eleven colored spots. Two yellow spots are from bumping into a lemonade stand. I had a lemonade stand once!" She draws the number symbol for numbers one through ten (with googly eyes) and then adds a big eleven at the top. Another student points to his drawing with five and says, "Here are three spots" *(circling the three spots on the dog's body with his pointer finger)*, "and here is one more" *(pointing to the spot on the ear just like the dog in the book)*, "and here is one more" *(pointing to a spot on the paw)*. He adds the equation 3 + 1 + 1 to his drawing. This open-ended Idea Investigation allows students to create their own drawings (with a unique number of spots) to match their dog's adventure story, and to write their stories as descriptive narratives, some with mathematical equations. By listening to their ideas and collecting their drawings to study, Mr. Collins learns a great deal about his students' thinking and how they are making sense of quantity and number symbols as well as their emerging understandings about addition equations.

My Bus (Barton 2014)

In this book, as the bus driver drives his bus to town, dogs and cats get on and off. The playful and colorful images in this story are ripe for mathematical noticings of all kinds! Younger children readily begin counting by ones to tell the number of animals, compare numbers, and sort and classify animals into categories of cats and dogs. "There are 1, 2, 3, 4, 5 cats on the bus! There is one dog on the bus. There are *more* cats than dogs on the bus!" says Ben.

While reading this story with a Math Lens, Mr. Perez's second-grade students make use of the clear action in the story, as cats and dogs get on and off the bus, to think about addition and subtraction. Mr. Perez wants to support his students in continuing to think about representing and solving addition and subtraction problems (noticing students tended to be most comfortable solving problems with numbers in the late teens and early twenties). He also sees the potential for students to work with equal groups of animals to support their emerging ideas about multiplication (similar to the investigation for *Dog's Colorful Day* described previously). Placing an illustration from the book under the document camera (Figure 6.25), Mr. Perez invites students to create an equation to match the picture and record their equations on their whiteboards.

Figure 6.25
My Bus Illustration

After engaging in discussion about their equations for the illustration, Mr. Perez invites students to create their own bus drawing. Students decide how many seats are on their bus, what types of animals and combination of animals get on and off the bus, and how to represent their story idea through drawings, equations, and sentences.

City Shapes (Murray 2016)

In Chapter 4, we noticed and wondered about an illustration in this vibrant story. After sharing this story with their students, Ms. Montagner and Mr. Henry (who teach multiage kindergarten and first-grade classes next door to one another) collaboratively design an Idea Investigation. Inspired by the shapes students noticed within the city in the story, they take their students on a field trip to walk around their school's urban neighborhood to look for shapes. Carrying clipboards with blank paper and a pencil (tied to the clipboard with brightly colored yarn), children look up in to the sky to see rectangular high-rise buildings with arrays of windows. They look down to discover hexagonal tiles on the bus depot floor. They take a rest and notice the benches are a series of 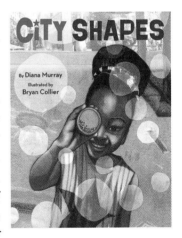 long rectangular metal pieces with round bolts holding them together. Exclaiming their discoveries and sketching them on their papers, students are overheard recognizing, identifying, and drawing a variety of shapes.

The teachers especially enjoy listening to the words the children use to describe their noticings. For example, while pointing to a telephone pole and tracing its height into the air with his finger, Samir describes, "This circle is tall! It is like lots of circles in a stack." Talia adds on, "Like a super tall stack of pancakes!" Mr. Henry comes alongside these young mathematicians to enjoy their noticing. "Wow, I wish I could eat a stack of pancakes that tall! Mathematicians call a tall circle like this a cylinder." He appreciates the emerging opportunities to notice and describe two-dimensional and three-dimensional shapes. He sketches a note of the students' names on his own clipboard and jots down that these children's ideas warrant further group discussion about identifying two-dimensional shapes as "flat" and three-dimensional shapes as "solid."

Meanwhile a group of children is gathered at a map, noticing the interesting and unusual shapes created in an aerial view of the city streets. Students talk over one another, sharing their noticings: "This shape is all pointy and it has 1, 2, 3, 4, 5 sides," "The sides are all straight lines," and "The sides are all different lengths." As Ms. Montagner listens in, she can hear her students describe the properties of a polygon. She jots a note to herself to bring these students' thinking about sides, lines, and lengths into their post-walk discussion.

As they head back toward the school, both teachers mention to each other that they overheard students describing objects in their city and the relative positions of these objects using words such as *next to, below, behind, in front of, way above*. The teachers are thrilled by the range of ideas that students are surfacing in this investigation and name that they enjoyed the city as a classroom community too. The teachers agree to come together after school that day to reflect on the shapes walk and collaboratively plan how to use the students' noticings, sketches, and ideas in a whole-class discussion the next day that might include a shared writing activity to generate a story of the students' experience on their neighborhood shape walk.

Round Is a Tortilla (Thong 2015)

Similar to *City Shapes*, this book's playful story context supports young mathematicians to see and think about shapes in their world (Figure 6.26). While sharing this story, Mr. Robertson and his second-grade students chart what they notice and wonder. Students notice round sombreros, the moon, trumpets, and campanas. They see rectangles in the ice-cream carts and stone metates (grinding stones). They find slices of watermelon and quesadillas are triangles. They wonder how shapes are the same and how they are different. Specifically, they wonder how a square and rectangle are the same and different.

Figure 6.26
Round Is a Tortilla Illustration

Flipping back through the illustrations in the story, Mr. Robertson remembers what it sounded like as students reasoned and argued about their ideas.

"Squares and rectangles both have four corners."

"They both have four sides."

"The sides are all straight."

"The corners are all like this *(holding two hands to make a ninety-degree angle)*."

"Yeah, but a rectangle looks flatter."

"Yes, like someone stepped on it *(stomping down)*!"

"Or squeezed it *(squishing hands together)*!"

As Mr. Robertson replays his students' words and actions, he chuckles as he is reminded of the power of gestures and how young mathematicians can show their emerging ideas with their hands and feet (before they may have the mathematical words) in such clever ways. He is inspired by the students' debate over the features of squares and rectangles and wants to design an investigation to support their careful noticing and thoughtful naming of properties of shapes. He decides the next day he will invite students to select any two shapes from the story and engage in their own noticing about how the shapes are the same and how they are different.

As the investigation experience plays out, students use everyday objects from the classroom (such as a book to represent a rectangle or a paper plate to resemble a circle), as well as mathematical manipulatives and tools, to model and reason about shapes and their attributes. Through the process of studying the details of shapes, creating drawings, and writing arguments for how their selected shapes are similar and different, students generate ideas about symmetry, line arcs, angle sizes, and numbers of faces. They play with rotation and partition shapes into equal portions. As they work toward more precise definitions, Mr. Robertson hears his students' emerging understandings about categories and subcategories.

An exciting outcome from this investigation happens when the students' conversation about squares and rectangles comes full circle! Through their investigation, students sharpen their noticings and claims:

Amir: All rectangles and all squares have four "page corner angles" (*holding a piece of construction paper to each of the corners to measure and prove ninety degrees*).

Sandra: All rectangles and squares have four straight-line sides.

Dennis: The lines of a square are all the same length. The lines of a rectangle are two different lengths. Two are longer, two are shorter.

Sandra: The lines of the rectangles that are running the same way (*gesturing with her hands to show parallel lines going vertically and then horizontally*) are the same length.

Terumi: A square is always, like, the same no matter how big or small, but a rectangle can be tall and skinny or short and bulgy.

Mr. Robertson can hear that students are on the cusp of an important mathematical noticing—all squares are rectangles but not all rectangles are squares. He cannot wait for students to make this discovery as they investigate further!

The Snowy Day (Keats 1962)

While enjoying this story with her first-grade students, Ms. Warme notices the illustration with footprints in the snow and thinks to herself, "This image would be a perfect opportunity to practice counting! I'm going to go back to this page tomorrow and invite students to count the footprints!" She recognizes the image as an opportunity for students to count and also for her to listen to their counting strategies.

The next day, Ms. Warme brings the book back out. As children gather on the carpet, she says, "Yesterday, as we were sharing this story together, I noticed an illustration that I want to look at together, again." Ms. Warme places the illustration under the document camera and invites the children to consider how they might count the footprints. After giving students a few moments to consider their ideas independently, Ms. Warme facilitates an open strategy share discussion in which students share and hear a wide range of counting strategies. Students count the footprints by 1s, by 2s, by 5s. Students count in 2 sets of 5 to make 10, and by 10s (Figure 6.27).

Figure 6.27
Students Count Footprints by Fives and Tens

Ms. Warme extends the discussion by inviting children to draw (on blank paper) or build (using cubes) their own snowy day footprints. She asks students to count their footprints, show their total, and write an equation to match their drawing or building. Some children draw animal footprints and count the toes.

Aimee: My dog walked in the snow! She has four toes on each paw and she has four paws. And she walked *aaaalll* the way down the street! So here are 1, 2, 3, 4 *(circling one paw)* and here are 1, 2, 3, 4 *(circling another paw)* . . . it's a lot of toes!

Lanh: My cat would *never* walk in the snow. He only likes to be cozy in his blanket!

Ivan: I walked with my dad in the snow. Here are his footprints, here are mine. His are bigger.

As often happens with open-ended tasks, students surprise Ms. Warme with the ways they approach the footprint investigation, and as they excitedly share their ideas she listens and learns a great deal about their creative thinking and mathematical reasoning.

Jabari Jumps (Cornwall 2017)

The children in Ms. Gray's second-grade class, whom we first met in Chapters 1 and 2, continue to read and think about *Jabari Jumps*. Through multiple reads, they deepen their connections to Jabari's feelings as he stands on the edge of the swimming pool's high dive. Students recognize the powerful feeling of being brave. They identify with how Jabari feels as he excitedly looks at the diving board from a distance, ready to try something new. They know just how he feels as he stands cautiously beneath the tall ladder of the diving board, pausing to allow other children to go in front of him in line. They root for Jabari as he courageously climbs up the tall ladder and walks to the edge of the board, curling his toes around

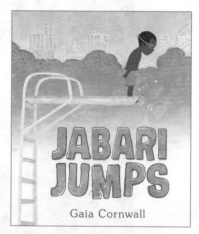

Gaia Cornwall

the tip while taking a deep breath. They share his excitement as Jabari springs off the board and plunges into the pool. They know how he feels as he pops up out of the water smiling, exclaiming, "I did it!" and walks back to the ladder to jump again!

Ms. Gray's class discussions about the story (before, during, and after the multiple reads) have narrowed upon studying Jabari's character. The students notice how brave Jabari is as he persists with courage.

"He is brave."

"He is trying something new and he is scared."

"The board is really high. He is going to go really deep in the water from jumping way up high."

As they wondered about how Jabari is able to try something new in the midst of being scared, especially with such a high diving board and going so deep into the water, their noticings are mathematical in nature and evoke wonder about the relationship between feelings, height, and depth.

The students also study Jabari's father. They notice how his dad supports him with affirmation, encouragement, and patience. Telling Jabari, "It's okay to feel a little scared," and "I take a deep breath and tell myself I'm ready . . . Sometimes it stops feeling scary and feels a little like a surprise." The second graders wonder about the role others play in supporting them when they have the scary feeling and, on the flip side, what role they may play in providing support to other people, like their classmates.

As an Idea Investigation, Ms. Gray chooses to pursue students' thinking about Jabari's persistence and to make connections to the mathematical practice of perseverance. Several times recently, the idea of perseverance had bubbled up in the students' mathematical discussions. They are learning that mathematicians stick with problems, especially when problems are challenging. They are learning that mathematics is about much more than speed and accuracy, and that the feeling of struggle can be exciting (and exhausting). The students are solving complex problems that stretch across multiple days and even weeks.

To launch the extension, Ms. Gray names the perseverance practices students have been engaged in, recapping their ideas about Jabari's stick-to-itiveness, and asks them, "How do you think perseverance and courage are connected?" After a few moments of individual thinking and writing time, she adds another layer to the extension, prompting, "Describe a time when you persevered as a mathematician. What helped you stick with it and what is something that someone else did, or said, that helped you persist?"

Students have time to write, share in small groups, and debrief with the whole class. Over the course of these discussions, they add depth and complexity to their definition of perseverance and make connections between their experiences as mathematicians, Jabari's courage, and his father's support:

Ashlinne: When a problem is hard, and I don't know the answer, or if I'm even on the right track, I have to be courageous and say, "I'm not sure yet." I have to trust that my classmates will support me and not make fun of me.

Eli: It takes courage to say you're scared, and it can feel scary to not know something!

Kyle: One time when I was struggling to find a solution, Felipe told me to keep going. He said he can feel frustrated, too. It reminds me of Jabari's dad.

Through these discussions of an idea-enhancing book, students are developing norms as a group of mathematicians who persevere individually and collectively.

Idea Investigations are meant to help students continue to think about and explore their questions as well as the mathematical and literary concepts that arise through read-alouds and discussion. Investigations are joyful and creative experiences that encourage unique perspectives, problem solving, and complex thinking. At the same time, investigations should be easy to plan, quick to prepare with simple or on-hand materials, and engaging in nature for both teacher and student. We encourage you to try on and innovate with investigations like these examples with your students in connection with reading aloud a work of children's literature.

Reflection and Discussion Questions

As you finish reading this chapter, here are some reflection questions for you to consider on your own or with colleagues:

1. As I practice planning for meaningful and creative Idea Investigations, what are some ways to connect literary and mathematical ideas raised through read-alouds to the experiences I am planning?

2. As I try out different Idea Investigations, what do I notice about the student discussion and learning opportunities afforded by open-ended tasks and challenging prompts?

3. What classroom or school resources do I have to help make Idea Investigations meaningful and engaging? These resources could include paper, crayons, pastels, paint (water color and/or tempera), math manipulatives (two-color counters, snap cubes, Unifix cubes, ten-frames), construction paper and tagboard for scenes and shadow puppets, recording devices for reader's theater, graph paper, geoboards, and classroom or outside spaces for creative play and movement.

Chapter 7
Learning Together as Educators

> **Schools should be organized for educators' learning as much as for students' learning.**
> —Elham Kazemi, Professor of Mathematics Education

Collaboratively planning for mathematizing read-aloud experiences with colleagues is a powerful opportunity to learn together as educators. Let's peek into a conversation among a couple of grade-level colleagues and an instructional coach as they plan a read-aloud together. The two first-grade teachers, Mr. Warfield and Ms. Wilson, and their coach, Ms. Bartlett, are sitting at a round table in the back of the classroom. They each brought children's literature to share. They've also gathered blank copies of the planning templates, sticky notes, a container of pencils, and an easel with chart paper and markers to help them get started.

Mr. Warfield: I asked Ms. Roberts (the school librarian) to share any new stories that she is excited or curious about with us. Here are the ones she suggested that our team use *(setting the books in the center of the table)*.

Ms. Wilson: Oh! I've been wanting to read this story *(reaching for a book she recognizes in the middle of the stack)*. I also pulled some stories from a recent book order that arrived that I haven't had time to look through yet. And collected a few books I think may be a part of our upcoming science and social studies units *(adding them to the pile)*.

Ms. Bartlett: This is exciting! We rarely get time to thumb through stories together. As we begin by exploring the stories ourselves, as readers and mathematicians, I've put our guiding questions on chart paper *(pulling the easel near)*. These can help us remember to ask ourselves, "What do *I* notice?" and "What do *I* wonder?" as *we* enjoy the stories.

As the three educators each reach for stories, they settle in and begin browsing individually. At times a gasp or a chuckle can be overheard. In other moments, a teammate can be seen sketching a thought on a sticky note and adding it to a page in a book. Taking time to read, as a part of the planning process, is a rare treat. And yet, it is becoming a common aspect and treasured element of their collaborative planning time. After about ten minutes, Ms. Bartlett begins writing on the easel as Mr. Warfield and Ms. Wilson finish the stories they are reading.

Ms. Bartlett: As you were reading, I sketched out the stages of our co-planning today (see Figure 7.1). We are already underway with the first step, exploring books as readers and mathematicians ourselves. Next, let's share what we noticed and wondered about in the stories we each read and surface the mathematical opportunities in each story! Then, let's collaboratively select which story we want to focus on and which type of read we want to begin with. After that, we can delve into co-planning for that story using a planning template.

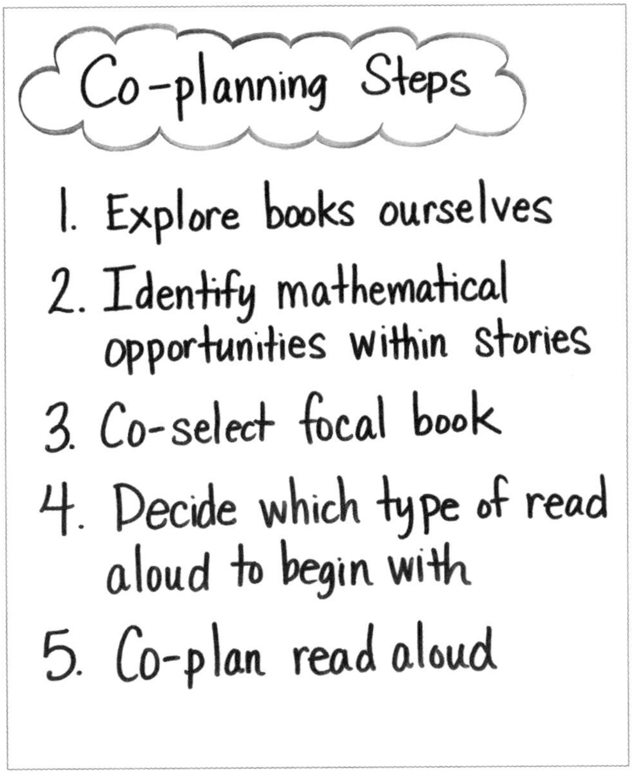

Co-planning Steps

1. Explore books ourselves
2. Identify mathematical opportunities within stories
3. Co-select focal book
4. Decide which type of read aloud to begin with
5. Co-plan read aloud

Figure 7.1
Co-Planning Steps

As the team of colleagues engages in the collaborative planning process, they share aloud excerpts and illustrations from stories that capture their interest. As each story is shared, they playfully brainstorm all the mathematical ideas that story context and illustrations might surface for children. They pull in some planning tools, such as state standards and the district pacing guide, that help them think about which mathematical content and practices they want students to have opportunities to think about. They also hold themselves open to meaningful mathematical opportunities that may lie outside predetermined standards or content aimed for their grade level. They walk the fine line of supporting their students to have sensemaking opportunities about the ideas they are studying while also seeking out opportunities for the beauty and curiosity of mathematics for mathematics' sake!

The team puzzles together over which book to read and why and which kind of read to begin with. After selecting the focal story, they decide to start with an Open Notice and Wonder read-aloud to get inside the story context and hear children's ideas. They plan to read aloud in their individual classrooms and Ms. Bartlett, the instructional coach, will join each discussion to record children's ideas and be a thought partner in the teaching and learning. The team decides they will bring the charted ideas to their next meeting, and from those ideas, they will decide which read to do next and why.

Engaging in Professional Learning Communities

Engaging in learning communities within our places of work is one way we grow as professional educators. Learning with colleagues tends to happen through various forms of professional learning communities, or PLCs. Lieberman and Miller describe PLCs as "places in which teachers pursue clear, shared purposes for student learning, engage in collaborative activities to achieve their purposes, and take collective responsibility for student learning" (1999, 53). If there are established PLCs in your work context, perhaps mathematizing children's literature can tap into and deepen those communities. Or, perhaps collaborative planning for and reflection of mathematizing can help build and grow a PLC in your school, whether with one willing partner or with a group of colleagues.

When taking up and learning through the ideas in this book, we envision professional learning in a range of collaborative contexts, from pairs of educators co-planning together to grade-level teams studying student work samples to school-wide professional learning initiatives pursuing systemic change. We view these diverse collaborative learning activities as variations of the PLC. Although PLCs may focus their work on supporting children's learning, learning communities also offer powerful opportunities to support educators' learning. Just like children's learning, educators' learning is dynamic, interactive, and ongoing. Research has identified a set of common practices for PLCs that we have found essential, including:

- Shared leadership
- Collaborative structures and relationships
- Continuous inquiry and learning over time
- Job-embedded learning within practice
- Focus on student learning as the desired outcome (Hord 1997)

The collaborative nature of PLCs and an ongoing focus on educators and children's learning are key factors in making professional learning experiences powerful and meaningful.

What Kinds of PLC Structures and Activities Can Support Educator Learning?

We have seen many PLC structures in practice when educators work together to mathematize children's literature. All of the structures work well with mathematizing literature, especially since reading aloud to children is a familiar and widespread instructional practice. In the following table, we have brainstormed PLC structures and mathematizing activities to spur your thinking. Many of the activities mentioned could work within any of the PLC structures (Figure 7.2).

Across the PLC structures listed in Figure 7.2, there are many different kinds of participants who could take part in the professional learning. PLC members might include classroom teachers, instructional assistants, school librarians, administrators, instructional coaches, district curriculum specialists, and teacher educators from partnering universities. Each participant brings expertise with them to the PLC. An instructional coach, for example, brings knowledge of curriculum, standards, and instructional practice, while a school administrator brings an understanding of school-wide student data, instructional trends, and connections to the local community. Different members in a PLC might also participate in the learning process in different ways. An instructional coach, for example, might take part in an Open Notice and Wonder read alongside the classroom teacher charting children's ideas and asking clarifying questions as part of the read-aloud and discussion (just as Ms. Bartlett plans to do in the opening vignette in this chapter). A principal might take the lead in enacting a read-aloud so that classroom teachers can observe, listen to, and focus on children's thinking. These opportunities bring educational leaders into the learning process as a participant rather than as an observer (or evaluator).

PLC Structure	PLC Activities
Educator Co-Planning	Two educators form a pair with an ongoing cycle of learning focused on co-selecting books, co-planning Open Notice and Wonder, Math Lens, and/or Story Explore reads, and collaboratively debriefing after trying the read-alouds in their classrooms (Joyce and Showers 1980; Showers and Joyce 1996).
Teams	Teams (grade level and/or cross grade level) co-plan read-alouds keeping curriculum materials, school district requirements, and state standards in mind; peer observations and collaborative teaching are possible activities if schedules allow.
School-Wide	Groups of educators, similar to grade-level teams in structure, join together school-wide to collaboratively plan, enact, and reflect on mathematized read-alouds and discussion. A principal and/or instructional coach may participate in the learning.
District-Level	Sometimes school-wide PLCs are part of a larger school district structure of professional learning where supports are provided across an entire district. Such professional learning opportunities sometimes include centralized PLC meetings coordinated by district curriculum specialists or instructional coaches and provide educators with opportunities to learn together with educators from other district sites and roles.

Figure 7.2
PLC Structures

Across PLC structures and the range of participants within them, we find power in the ongoing nature of these communities as a way to create lasting change and to improve instructional practice while also impacting school-wide student learning. With learning as the central purpose of PLCs—both learning of children and learning of educators—there is a sense of growth and a feeling of positivity that help motivate and sustain our work.

What Can PLCs Learn Through Mathematizing?

As educators, we are always learning—this is one of the best parts of our profession! Mathematizing opens up opportunities for educators to work on a wide range of knowledge and skills in teaching. Through mathematizing literature, PLCs can deepen knowledge of teaching and learning in mathematics and literacy. PLCs can also study complex practices that educators enact, such as asking open-ended questions, engaging children in productive struggle, and planning for and facilitating discussions. Let's think more deeply about what it can look like (and sound like) to learn with our colleagues through mathematizing.

Deepening knowledge of mathematical ideas and concepts

Coming to know the mathematics we teach, and how children think about those ideas over time, is an important part of our work as teachers of mathematics. It is also a gift that we have the opportunity to deepen our own mathematical understanding and grow our identity as mathematicians through the work of teaching. For me, Allison, the power of learning mathematics as an educator happened early in my career when I was a fifth-grade teacher. Learning alongside my students, using an inquiry-oriented curriculum, I began (*for the first time in my life!*) to understand mathematics. By this I mean really understanding why and how a strategy worked, rather than following a sequence of steps without reasoning. One evening I attempted to understand why it makes sense to invert and multiply when you're dividing fractions. I sketched representations with colored pencils and will never forget the surge of inspiration when I could see why this strategy works! My colleagues were generous as they listened to me try to use words to explain my emerging understanding with clunky enthusiasm. In that moment, I began identifying as a mathematician. In that year, I began to see math everywhere in the world around me. I began to recognize the beauty and the playful nature of mathematics.

Teaching mathematics with and for understanding, beyond rules and procedures, means continually developing our own mathematical thinking and sense of self. Through mathematizing we have the chance to more deeply understand the math we teach and to nurture our identity as a mathematician. For example, think back to the story *Full House: An Invitation to Fractions* (Dodds 2009) written about in Chapters 3 and 6. In Chapter 6, during an idea investigation after reading the story, Mr. Llorente and his class grappled with ideas about adding fractions. When students generated the conjecture that $\frac{5}{6} + \frac{1}{6} = \frac{6}{12}$ (referring to the context of the filled rooms at the inn), an opportunity for sense making about combining portions emerged for students and for Mr. Llorente. In hearing and responding to this conjecture (both in the moment and afterward), Mr. Llorente had the opportunity to deepen his conceptual understanding about combining portions, defining the whole, and how and why it matters that the whole can change. These are complex ideas to understand when teaching and learning about fractions. Through a story context, like the inn with six rooms, we can use the story and illustrations to help us think, alongside students, as mathematicians.

Questions to guide learning about mathematical ideas and concepts:

- Which mathematical ideas and/or concepts could be explored through this story?

- Which mathematical ideas might student notice and wonder about? How might those ideas relate to our current units of study? How might those ideas be connected to other important mathematical learning beyond our current unit of study?

- How can exploration of mathematical ideas through this story support students' learning of content?

- In what ways could we, as educators, deepen our understanding of content?

- What do we understand about this content? What are we coming to understand about this content? What does not yet make sense about this content?

- What are we learning about how children's understanding of content develops over time?

Deepening knowledge of mathematical practices

As teachers of mathematics, we also know it is important to support children to *think like mathematicians*. For math practices, we shift from focusing on content, or what we want mathematicians to know, to thinking about what we want mathematicians to be able to do. Mathematicians do many things! They make sense of problems and persevere in solving them, they reason, they argue, they justify, they model and make use of structure. We listened to children do this with Ms. Gannon in Chapter 6 when they argued—or worked on constructing viable arguments—against the author with *This Is a Ball* (Stanton and Stanton 2017).

Through mathematizing, we can learn how to support children to think and act like mathematicians. We can also grow our own ability to think and act like mathematicians. For example, think back to the story *The Most Magnificent Thing* (Spires 2014) mentioned in previous chapters. In this story, the main character (a young engineer) travels through the iterative cycle of design. She tinkers, hammers, adjusts, and struggles to create something magnificent. In Chapter 5, we thought about what it could look like to facilitate a Math Lens read to focus on the young engineer's perseverance. Perseverance is an important practice for mathematicians. Yet, how do we study perseverance? How can we surface explicit discussion about persevering? Observing, describing, and analyzing the young engineer's experiences with the emotions of failure and iteration open up an opportunity to see a mathematician in action and discuss with children what it looks like, and feels like, to persevere. Through this story and the illustrations, we see that when a mathematician perseveres, she may feel mad, she may explode, she may experience her "not finest moment!" She may quit, she may need a walk, she may revise, she may discover something she didn't realize was possible. Learning ways mathematicians act is an important part of being a mathematician. Stories can help students and teachers work on a wide range of mathematical practices.

Questions to guide learning about mathematical practices include:

- Where do we see an opportunity to grow our understanding, and our students' understanding, of mathematical practices in an upcoming read-aloud? How may exploration of mathematical practices through this story support students as mathematicians?

- In what ways could we, as educators, deepen our understanding and enactment of mathematical practices?

- Which mathematical practices are we attending to in our work? Which mathematical practices do we need more opportunities to experience and learn in our community?

Deepening knowledge of stories

As teachers of literacy, we know it is important to support children in becoming active and motivated readers who think about what they read. We model how we think and how we make sense of what we are reading; we model this awareness, or self-monitoring, as we read aloud and invite children to join in discussion about the stories we are reading and experiencing together. For me, Tony, reading to children and thinking aloud to show them my own processes as a reader and how I make sense of stories is my most favorite thing to do. I pause and ask myself questions, notice ideas that are puzzling and that I wonder about, and exclaim when I find a new or interesting word that I jot down as vocabulary to be investigated later. I enjoy inviting children to join in to discuss words, questions, and ideas.

Through mathematizing, we can learn how to support children in becoming active and motivated readers who self-monitor as they read independently and construct meaning from text. Mathematizing lends itself to focusing on two major literacy domains of skill and knowledge: comprehension strategies and decoding/vocabulary skills.

Predicting story events and inferring the actions, thoughts, and feelings of characters are two comprehension strategies that fit most often with mathematized children's literature.

Who Sank the Boat? (Allen 1983), for example, lends itself to an exploration of predicting what will happen next as we try to determine which animal will sink the boat! We might ask, "What do you think will happen next? Will the cow sink the boat? Why do you think so?" *The Most Magnificent Thing* (Spires 2014) provides wonderful opportunities for children to predict what the girl is trying to make and what she will try next in her engineering process of creation. We might ask, "What do you think she is trying to make? What will she try next? What is a magnificent thing, and what do you think she will need to do to create it?"

Grumpy Bird (Tankard 2007) is an example of a story that works well for making inferences about characters and their actions. Bird stays grumpy throughout most of the book, while Bird's friends don't seem to notice his bad mood . . . or do they? Near the end of the book Bird is no longer grumpy; we might ask, "Why is Bird no longer grumpy? What changed? What is Bird's mood now, and how do we know?" *Last Stop on Market Street* (de la Peña 2015) provides similar inference opportunities, but with human characters in a realistic setting. We might ask, "How is CJ feeling? How do we know? When does he stop feeling sad, and how do we know?" Discussion around character actions and feelings and how we make inferences about them is a powerful way to explore how this particular comprehension strategy helps us more deeply comprehend a story.

Exploring mathematized stories together also helps us support children's decoding and vocabulary skills. Emergent readers need lots of practice with choral reading, predictable text, and high-frequency words to build automaticity in word identification. Books with high-frequency and decodable words, repeating patterns or phrases, and rhyme help children with decoding skills. Additionally, readers of all ages need exposure to, and discussion of, new vocabulary that will help grow not only their decoding skills but also their vocabulary knowledge, which helps deepen comprehension.

Quack and Count (Baker 1999) is an example of a story that has both decoding and vocabulary opportunities for exploration. It features rhyming text with a pattern that repeats, "7 ducklings, __ plus __," followed by a series of action words. Together this makes for easy memorization and fun wordplay with action words that include *slipping, sliding, chasing, quacking, playing, splashing, paddling, flapping,* and *reaching. Who Sank the Boat?* features the repeating question, "Do you know who sank the boat?" along with the phrase, "No, it wasn't the ___." This repetition encourages children to chime in and to discuss what they think about who will sink the boat. The book also features some really interesting vocabulary words to explore, such as *tilted, balanced, stepped,* and *level,* as well as relatively rare but interesting words like *din, bow* (of a boat), *flutter,* and *knit.* Children can discuss these words and come up with working definitions of them, based on their use in the story.

Wordless picture books like *Flashlight* (Boyd 2014) present an opportunity to assess children's abilities to apply comprehension strategies to a story as they generate their own narrative in their own words, perhaps using newly learned vocabulary in the process. In *Flashlight*, children could predict story events (either prompted or not) and infer what the child in the story might be thinking and feeling. This book also provides a good opportunity to listen for interesting vocabulary and math-related ideas or words that children might mention or weave into the story. Here are some examples of what two third-grade students said as they explored *Flashlight*:

Reid: I notice these holes on each page, and when you flip the page, they do something different. This circle is around a butterfly but on the next page it shows the moon. There are lots of berries on this tree. I would count the berries—that branch has four, that other branch has four, that one has two and that one has one. So, 4 plus 4 is 8, and 8 plus 2 is 10, and 10 plus 1 equals 11. I notice there's a bunch of apples lying around, and some are whole but some have bites missing.

Listening to Reid, we can hear that he is noticing the shape of the cutouts in the pages, and as he flips the pages, he sees what is within the view of the circle-shaped hole. He sees quantities—of berries and apples—and he sees items in groups—four berries, two berries. He combines groups as he adds, no longer counting all by ones. He sees which apples are whole and which have portions missing from animal bites. He sees this illustration with a mathematical lens.

Vanya: It looks like he found a house! Good thing he's not trespassing. I would not want to be out that late at night. He's looking at stuff and he's eating at night. He must be nocturnal. Then he tripped! That's like me when I go hiking! He dropped the flashlight. Before he wasn't in color, but now that the flashlight is shining on him, he is in color. I think the nighttime makes life look like TV shows, black and white. Now there are actually colors around; I am expecting it to be day soon. I'm not sure in real life if the animals will be able to hold a flashlight. Different animals are holding it!

Vanya's observations provide a wealth of information about how she is making sense of the story and making connections between the character's experience and her own; she indicates awareness of what makes something "nocturnal," considers visual elements and perspective between color and black and white, and hints at the issue of fantasy versus realistic fiction in this story.

Questions to guide learning about comprehension strategies and vocabulary:

- How might prediction help students comprehend the story, and where are good stopping points to ask what will happen next?

- What character traits and actions might be inferred from the story, and where are good stopping points to ask about the characters and their actions?

- What sight words or high-frequency words occur in the story, and how might we help readers decode them?

- What word patterns are prominent in the story, and how might we pause and discuss them?

- What repetitive words and phrases might scaffold children's decoding efforts, and what instructional moves might we use to encourage participation in reading the story together?

- What key vocabulary words are essential to understanding the story, and how might we pause to explore their meaning?

- What kinds of idea investigations might help children continue exploring comprehension strategies and decoding and vocabulary skills after the story is over?

Planning for and Enacting Complex Teaching Practices

As we collaboratively plan (and perhaps facilitate) with colleagues, one kind of learning we are doing is learning *how* to mathematize stories. As we've been focused on throughout this book so far, communities can learn how and why to select books, how to plan for and facilitate different reads of the same story, and how to plan meaningful idea investigations. Beyond learning how to mathematize, another way that educators learn together is to focus on complex aspects of teaching that are central to mathematizing and also live beyond mathematizing, such as asking open-ended questions, hearing and considering children's ideas, and engaging children in productive struggle. For example, as educators plan for mathematizing a story, we can help each other think about when and how to ask open-ended questions during discussions. We can sketch out what those questions might sound like on planning templates. We can practice asking open-ended questions during a discussion, and afterward reflect on whether or not our questions opened up opportunities to hear students' thinking. Or, as another example, educators can support each other to design opportunities for children to engage in productive struggle and grow our comfort with allowing children to be within struggle.

These complex practices are central to mathematizing, and they also have deep roots in our work as educators, spanning all disciplines across our days with children. As educators we are always striving to grow and deepen our ability to enact these complex parts of practice well.

Asking open-ended questions

Across an entire school day, and all the subjects we teach, asking open-ended questions is a powerful and important practice. Open-ended questions invite children to think and teachers to listen. Questions such as "Can you tell us more about your thinking?" allow us, as teachers, to listen to children's ideas and allow children to hear their own and other's ideas. Questions such as "Can you tell us why you think that is true?" or "What from the story is making you think that?" encourage children to reason about, justify, and explain their ideas—often using stories as contextual or supporting information. Asking questions with many or more than one "right" answer broadens participation by allowing *all* children to have and share an idea and engage in classroom discussions.

Open-ended questions come in many forms. Oftentimes we have questions we may ask in nearly any situation, such as "What do you notice?"; "How did you think about this problem?"; or "What do you think will happen next, and why do you think so?" In our mathematizing work, we call these "questions as refrain." We invite you to print and use the questions as refrain bookmark in Appendix B, play with these questions, and make them your own.

Open-ended questions may also be specific to the current discussion. For example, when reading and discussing an illustration in *The Snowy Day* (Keats 1962), we can ask, "How did you count the footprints?" Hearing children's strategies for counting the footprints allows us to hear the range of ways children are counting in our community (Are children counting by ones? Counting by twos or a different combination of numbers? Who is on the cusp of transitioning from counting *all* to counting *on*?) and engage in discussion that celebrates and advances young mathematicians' counting strategies in our community. Also, asking children to explain their strategy helps to make the mathematics visible and encourages reflection about and justification of ideas (National Council of Teachers of Mathematics 2014). Imagine asking children, "What might an equation look like to match your strategy?"

or "How might you prove there are thirty-two footprints?" These questions may prompt discussion of, and connections between, mathematical ideas and relationships. They may also encourage debate, such as the time we heard children argue for thirty footprints versus thirty-two footprints, depending on if the character's current holes for their feet counted as footprints or not!

We might ask similar kinds of questions when focusing on the story itself. When the girl engineer in *The Most Magnificent Thing* is so frustrated that a vortex forms above her head, one might ask, "How is she feeling, and why do you think so?" followed up by another open-ended question connecting the character's emotions to children's experiences, such as "Do you remember a time when you felt the same way? What was that like?" In this same story, a focus on the word *magnificent* itself is worthy of discussion. At a stopping point about halfway through the story, one might ask, "What is she trying to create? What *is* a magnificent thing?" This could be followed up with open-ended questions about the term *magnificent* after reading, encouraging children to come up with a working definition of the term based on story events.

Asking open-ended questions and listening carefully to decide what to ask next is challenging work. When I, Allison, was first learning how to facilitate discussions of students' mathematical ideas, our elementary school math coach, Mrs. Allen, gave me the gift of two widely versatile open-ended questions. On 3-by-5-inch note cards, she wrote the questions "How did you solve?" and "How do you know that?" I carried these cards on a clipboard, as I shifted from asking questions that had one right answer to beginning to ask questions that invited children to think and allowed me to hear their thinking. As I asked children to explain their ideas, they became used to justifying their answers. Over time, asking these questions had a snowball effect because I became insatiably curious about children's thinking and the children became curious about one another's ideas. They began asking each other, "How do you know that?" before I could ask. We all began listening to each other more deeply perhaps because there was something interesting to listen to! It is much more interesting to listen to another's reasoning rather than just their answer. Hearing children's ideas informed where we went next in our classroom discussions, revealed insights into what students understood and what they were coming to understand, and instantly became fodder for stories shared in the staff room and around the dinner table. "You cannot make this stuff up!" often followed the reiteration of children's quotes.

As you, and perhaps your PLC, play with asking more open-ended questions, here are some questions to consider:

- What do we notice about questions that open up versus shut down children's thinking?

- What kinds of questions provide opportunities for children to think about and share their ideas? What do these questions sound like?

- What are two open-ended questions I could experiment with to grow my practice?

- How do I tend to respond to the ideas that children share? How can I get better at asking a series of open-ended questions that continue to delve into a child's idea?

- How comfortable am I with wait time, to give children an authentic opportunity to think before responding to an open-ended question? What follow-up questions or prompts might I keep in mind if think time turns into puzzlement or prolonged silence?

- Where do I see an opportunity to practice posing open-ended questions in an upcoming read-aloud?

Engaging in productive struggle

Can you think of a time when you were on the cusp of understanding a new idea? Or a time when you began to have a new thought that was not yet fully formed? What do you remember about how you felt in these moments? Moments of disequilibrium can be thrilling and terrifying! Moments of uncertainty can also bring a wide range of emotions for educators and children. When struggle emerges, a child may become frustrated and give up. Educators may be tempted to rush in and make the task or problem easier or do the thinking for the child. Yet struggle is often essential to learning with understanding. The National Council of Teachers of Mathematics writes in *Principles to Actions*, "Effective teaching of mathematics consistently provides students, individually and collectively, with opportunities and supports to engage in productive struggle as they grapple with mathematical ideas and relationships" (2014, 48).

Through mathematizing children's literature, we can work purposefully on cultivating teaching and learning that involves *productive struggle*. Struggle is productive when children are grappling toward new understandings with ideas (National Council of Teachers of Mathematics 2014), resulting in increased skill, knowledge, and confidence. Struggle is unproductive when children are not progressing toward sense making, resulting in frustration and perhaps confirmation of a negative fixed mindset (Warshauer 2014). We can practice designing and enacting tasks that allow moments of productive struggle to emerge. We can learn more about how to support ourselves and children within moments of struggle, acknowledging that struggle takes time, space, and effort, which can sometimes be tense or uncomfortable. We can reframe perceptions of struggle, and what it looks like and sounds like, to persevere within and through struggle as mathematicians and readers.

Stories are powerful contexts for practicing teaching and learning that involve struggle. By offering a story as a thinking space and wrapping a story context around the questions and the problems we are solving, there are greater supports for sense making and learning with understanding. For example, in the story *Stack the Cats* (Ghahremani 2017), the cats prefer to stack in threes. Beyond three, stacks of cats begin to teeter and totter. When reading aloud from the part of this story in which eight cats try to form a stack and began to tumble, Ms. Wishart paused to ask her first-grade students the open-ended question, "How do you think the cats will land?" We both (Allison and Tony) remember a moment of quiet tension that hung over the room. Ms. Wishart turned to us to confer and consider if she should ask the question in a different way. She wondered if the way she asked the question made sense to the students. Did she need to ask a question that was more directive? Or were students quiet because they were thinking? We believed that students were thinking, and we decided to use extended wait time. Slowly, children began reaching for Unifix cubes, sketching on the whiteboards in their laps, or drawing on plain paper. As we knelt next to children to hear their ideas-in-progress, we were glad we chose to stick with the question (even though we felt uneasy for more than a few moments) and allow the struggle to emerge. These young students were neither confused nor off-task. They were thinking!

As Ms. Wishart's students continued to develop their ideas, and as they shared their thinking with the whole group, we could hear the ways this question opened up meaningful opportunities for young mathematicians to engage in sense making about mathematical content (e.g., the number sequence and combinations of eight or nine) and engage in mathematical practices (e.g., making sense of problems and persevering in solving them, modeling with mathematics, and looking for and making use of structure). We could hear the ways the story supported students within the struggle. As one child said, "I wasn't sure. But, on every page, there is a new cat. See, here in the book it goes 1 cat, 2 cats, 3 cats . . . so I knew after 8 cats there were going to be 9 cats. And if the cats like to be in stacks of three, that would be *(pointing to, and counting aloud, the Unifix cubes on her desk that represented the cats 1, 2, 3 and 4, 5, 6 and 7, 8, 9)* 9 cats or . . . 3 stacks." She quickly added on, "I wish I had nine cats at my house!"

Another student shared his drawing of eight cats standing on the ground and explained, "I think the cats will land like this *(pointing to the cats standing in his drawing, showing eight cats standing in a row)* because everybody knows that cats always land on their feet!" Both of these students' sense making was supported by the story as well as what they know from life experiences.

In reflecting on this episode, we thought about how Ms. Wishart's open-ended question "How do you think the cats will land?" created powerful opportunities for her students and for her. This open-ended question was powerful because there are many different ways children may approach, represent, and solve this problem with many possible answers. As children create their own solutions, they engage in complex thinking. Complex thinking can evoke struggle and can take considerable effort and time—and time to think is not something that occurs in classrooms without nurturing, encouragement, and support. For example, a child might grapple with how to begin, where to go next, how many ways might be true, how to explain their idea. A teacher might grapple with the ambiguity, understanding and supporting many solutions and strategies, allowing struggle to emerge and be alive, how to orient children to one another's ideas, and tapping into and growing her deep knowledge of children's thinking and mathematical content. These kinds of explorations involving productive struggle and the deep thinking that goes with it take lots of time— to think, problem solve, discuss, and reconsider. We believe this is time well spent, and we acknowledge it feels very different from the kinds of quick task-completion activities that might be more common in elementary classrooms.

What might it sound like for educators to purposefully plan for struggle? Let's peek into a planning conversation between two teachers as they work together to design an idea investigation after reading *Splash!* (Jonas 1997) with their second-grade students. Before meeting to plan together, both teachers had facilitated several reads of *Splash!* with their students. As the two teachers came together to plan for an idea investigation, they brought the chart papers from previous classroom discussions (showing students' ideas from an Open Notice and Wonder, a Story Explore, and a Math Lens read) and posted them on the wall. They also brought a few copies of the Idea Investigation planning template (see Appendix D), copies of the book, and some sticky notes and pencils.

Ms. Seretse: I'm wondering how we can use students' ideas from these previous discussions to design an idea investigation that allows for sense making *and* opens up opportunities for productive struggle.

Ms. Arias: I'm wondering that, too. I want to get better at planning for and asking questions that allow struggle to emerge, and I want to pay attention to how I respond when the struggle surfaces. I want to lean into the struggle, and I'm not always sure what to say or what to do!

Ms. Seretse: Same for me. It is one thing to plan for struggle, it is another thing to stick with it when it emerges! Let's use this idea investigation as an opportunity to try out a few new questions and plan some responses we can try when struggle happens.

With the shared goal of using children's ideas from previous discussions to inform purposeful planning of a task that will allow struggle to emerge, Ms. Arias and Ms. Seretse study children's ideas on the chart papers. As they look for themes across the posters, they use questions to guide their noticings: "What do we notice about our students' ideas?" "Where might we go next to deepen sense making?" "What type of task is open enough for struggle to emerge?" "How can we lean into the struggle?" They collaboratively design a task that will invite children to create their own pond and to write an equation that matches their drawing. They hope the open-ended nature of the task will provide broad access, will result in a range of ideas and solutions, and is purposefully ambiguous enough to allow for students to problem solve and hopefully get into some productive struggle. Ms. Arias and Ms. Seretse sketch out responses and questions to try if and when struggle comes up, including "Tell me more about your drawing"; "Where are you getting stuck?"; "Would any tools help you think?" (possibly offering the book or Unifix cubes); or "I can see you're really thinking, keep going!"

Questions to guide learning about enacting tasks to support productive struggle include the following:

- What are some features of mathematical tasks that allow children to think deeply and wrestle with complex ideas?

- What would it look like to design a mathematizing task that promotes reasoning and problem solving?

- What tools may support students' thinking when they are engaged in productive struggle?

- What might I say, or what moves might I make, to support students' continued thinking and reasoning?

- How can I help students learn how to explain their thinking in the midst of struggle?

- How can I help students to learn how to support each other in moments of struggle? What would that sound like for me and for them?

- How might engaging in productive struggle shape students' identities as mathematicians?

Common Wonderings from Educators

We've found that as teachers think and plan together around mathematizing read-alouds, some important questions begin to emerge. In the following section, we share our take on those questions, but you may adapt and come to your own conclusions based on your own experiences. What really matters is that we maintain a focus on the joy and wonder of children's ideas and using stories as a meaningful context to support young readers and mathematicians.

When might a mathematized read-aloud occur during the school day and why?

One question we often hear from teachers is "Should I mathematize stories during reading time or math time?" This is a question we have pondered, too. Teaching within an elementary school day provides us with some flexibility to make decisions about what is taught when. You may choose to plan a read-aloud and discussion to occur during your literacy block or during math time, depending on the flow of the day and which discussion structure you're enacting. Although it may tend to make sense to plan for a Story Explore read during a literacy block or a Math Lens read within math time, it can also be powerful to purposefully have a Math Lens read-aloud and discussion during a literacy block or vice versa to help children, and ourselves, remember that meaningful learning is integrated and happens across disciplines. You may also find a few moments to sneak in a read-aloud or book or illustration exploration before or after recess or in times of transition. If you are participating in a PLC that involves team planning and time to be in each other's classrooms, scheduling a read-aloud that works with these collaborative activities is also important. The more moments we can create for delving into a story and thinking like mathematicians, the better!

How might I plan for a sequence of read-alouds that span a week, a month, or a unit?

Another consideration when planning beyond the lesson level is to consider what a sequence of lessons may look like across a week, a couple weeks, a month, or a longer unit of study. Across Chapters 4–6, we saw how teachers enacted a sequence of read-alouds and discussions across a week. Ms. Hadreas chose to sequence the multiple reads of *Last Stop on Market Street*, beginning with an Open Notice and Wonder, followed by a Story Explore, and ending with a Math Lens read. Similarly, Ms. Burris chose to sequence read-alouds with *The Lion's Share* (McElligott 2012) by also beginning with an Open Notice and Wonder, yet she then facilitated a Math Lens, and finally a Story Explore read. Both of these sequences spanned a week but could have spanned two weeks or more (especially when including idea investigations).

As you think about book selection, on your own or while planning with colleagues, you could consider the question: What might a sequence of stories look like and why? Perhaps you could map out a sequence of stories that allows you to delve more deeply into a mathematical idea as you make plans for an upcoming unit. We might, for example, plan the following sequence of stories across two weeks: *Who Sank the Boat?*, *Quack and Count*, and *Stack the Cats* to engage in sense making about increasingly large number combinations, from five to seven to ten. As you look across the mathematical ideas in the unit, you could think about when you might read a story and why. You may be selecting that sequence of stories because they form an intentional string of experiences in terms of mathematical concepts, literary ideas, or both. The challenge is to think beyond text-dependent books and remember to allow space for children to drive the mathematical noticing and wonder and exploration. Flexibility is key.

How might I engage in a planned read-aloud while also remaining responsive to emerging ideas I didn't anticipate?

Teachers give careful thought when planning for read-alouds. We thoughtfully select a story and mark stopping points to pause for questions and discussion. We anticipate what children might say and we sketch questions we aim to pose. However, we all know enactments of our plans rarely transpire exactly how we anticipated! This is a joy and challenge of teaching that keeps us on our toes.

While reading, we try to stay open to ideas that are interesting and exciting to children, whether or not we noticed or wondered about these ideas ourselves. This is easier to do with an Open Notice and Wonder read than it might be for a more focused Story Explore or Math Lens read. Listening to children is crucial. As we listen to what they notice, what they wonder, and what ideas they share, we may choose to pause and revise our plans to keep children's questions at the center of our work. Or maybe a different spontaneous opportunity arises when children begin to mathematize a story that you didn't plan to read aloud or that you didn't plan to approach as mathematicians. We have found that these opportunities arise more frequently when a group of children has gained experience with mathematizing and the students are excited to see mathematics in any book being shared or that is available in the classroom library. When unplanned mathematizing occurs, we know mathematizing has taken hold in our classroom!

In these moments when children take us in a direction we did not anticipate, we can face the challenge of pursuing children's ideas while keeping an eye on our goals for a lesson. Mathematizing stories provides fruitful opportunities to be curious about this challenge in the teaching profession and to learn with and from colleagues about how to think about and navigate these experiences. We acknowledge the tension between listening to and following children's ideas and pushing ahead with our own teaching and learning goals.

What in-the-moment decisions might I make based on children's ideas and discussion?

Skilled teachers are adaptive (Duffy 2004), responding to unexpected moments in thoughtful ways to further children's thinking, engage children with their own and each other's ideas, and position children competently. In an Open Notice and Wonder read, for example, we have learned to expect the unexpected since we are, to some degree, asking for it! Sometimes a student will notice or wonder about something we had never thought of, no matter how familiar we are with the story. For example, one boy noticed that at the end of *Who Sank the Boat?* the mouse managed to stay dry while all of the other animals got wet. We had never noticed this before! In this moment we had to decide: Do we chart his idea? Do we ask a follow-up question such as "Why might the mouse not have gotten wet?" Do we acknowledge his noticing and move on? We decided to chart his idea (as a way to allow him and his classmates to engage with his noticing and position him competently) and continue reading and discussing the story. We imagined that his idea might provide an opportunity for further exploration during a Math Lens read another day focused on balance, size, or number.

Sometimes during a Math Lens or Story Explore read, an unexpected moment might change the focus and direction of the entire read-aloud discussion. In these instances, we must remain adaptive and decide in the moment whether to pursue what is likely a new idea or to stay on course with our original plan. This decision for us is based on learning—which direction will help children learn the most right now, in this moment? Which lesson is the most needed or important in our community right now? There is always a learning, be it academic (e.g., weight effects balance) or social (e.g., your ideas matter here). For example, near the end of her Story Explore read of *Last Stop on Market Street*, a student surprised Ms. Hadreas by declaring that CJ and Nana were at the soup kitchen to make money to buy a car. In that moment, to help clarify this story development, Ms. Hadreas decided to ask unplanned follow-up questions to hear more about this student's current thinking and hear other children's ideas about what CJ and Nana were doing in the soup kitchen, which though clearly illustrated was not described or identified as such in the text of the story. She said, "That is a good point you're bringing up that we should think more about why Nana and CJ are at the soup kitchen. Let's think more about that, together." Ms. Hadreas asked, "Why might they be helping and serving? How does CJ feel now? What do you think?"

One student replied, "I think they are cooking for the other people. He looks like he feels helpful and glad."

Another student added, "They are giving some people in their community something to eat. CJ and Nana are poor too and they are helping other people who are their neighbors." With these responses, Ms. Hadreas could begin to hear children were developing a deeper understanding of CJ and Nana's actions as well as the purpose of a soup kitchen, something she originally thought they might already know. Ms. Hadreas was careful to engage with this child's current interpretation of the story. She took up his idea and positioned him as raising a matter worth discussing, rather than correcting him or dismissing his current idea. Her adaptive teaching during this unexpected moment helped steer the discussion toward new understandings without her having to declare a "right answer" and possibly shutting down the discussion.

When we listen to children, honor their current ideas and their ideas-in-progress, and position them competently, we must be prepared to be adaptive teachers who explore what children are thinking about in addition to what we may have planned or deemed important. This can feel a bit unsettling, at least at first, but it is also freeing (we don't need to know every detail all the time) and empowering (children feel listened to and more eager to share). Children will surprise us with their thoughtful noticings and wonderings and their insightful discussion points. As teachers we listen to children, encourage them to share their ideas, and create time and space for meaningful discussion to occur.

When reflecting (on your own or with other educators) after the read-aloud, what can we learn about children's ideas?

The process of mathematizing read-alouds generates different kinds of artifacts for assessment, reflection, and planning. We encourage educators to consider the following artifacts when reflecting on teaching and learning on your own or with colleagues after working with children.

ARTIFACTS
- Sketched-in templates
- Charted ideas
- Student work
- Book with sticky notes in it
- Pile of books to consider

Taking the time to look through and consider mathematizing artifacts can help us see what ideas and concepts children do understand, might be actively making sense of and coming to understand, and/or are asking questions about. We can then use what we notice from the artifacts to guide future instruction and discussions. Let's return to the example of the idea investigation vignette after reading and discussing *Full House: An Invitation to Fractions*. As Mr. Llorente and his students engaged in that heated debate about whether five full guest rooms plus the room for the innkeeper would equal a full house ($\frac{5}{6} + \frac{1}{6} = \frac{6}{6} = 1$), what did we hear these children understand? Studying the charted ideas from discussion (and examining students' drawings and equations) helped us to hear and see that these children were coming to understand parts of a whole and could think flexibly about decomposing and recomposing portions. We could also hear and see there may be some emerging thinking about the whole and how and why the whole changes within this context when adding portions. Relying on the context of the guest rooms in this story gave us more in-depth insights into what these children understood and were coming to understand, which helped Mr. Llorente decide where to go next in their studies of fractions. He decided to have a subsequent discussion that asked students to reason about each fraction in their equation, and what it represented in the story, and to press for reasoning and sense making about combining fifths and sixths.

Children's wonderings and questions also provide opportunities for further exploration of ideas and emerging thinking. With a book like *Hooray for Fish* (Cousins 2017), a brightly colored illustration-exploring book introduced briefly in Chapter 3, we find that charted lists of children's wonderings provide ideas for additional explorations. For example, when children ask questions such as "Which is bigger, the seahorse or the orange fish in the center?," we can ask, "Which do you think is bigger?" and "How do you know?" Or if a child asks, "How many dots are on that fish?," we can ask, "How many dots do you see on the brown stingray? How do you see them?" With an eye on pattern, we might explore a bit further by asking, "What patterns do you see, and how would you describe them?" Planning future reads, both revisiting the same book and exploring others, is an exciting endeavor when building on children's interests and curiosity. Pausing during and after discussions to study children's ideas helps us make decisions about where to steer our learning.

What did I learn from the read-aloud experience, and what might I work on next?

Reflecting on our own learning is another important step in the process, one that we can both consider individually and discuss in PLCs.

Questions to guide reflecting on read-aloud experiences include the following:

- What went well, and how do I know this?

- What about the read-aloud experience surprised me?

- What about the experience did I find challenging?

- How did children respond to the read-aloud?

- How did I feel about incorporating math ideas into a read-aloud?

- How did I do with stopping points and questions?

- If I did an idea investigation, what was that like? How did it go? Was this investigation clearly connected to ideas highlighted in the read-aloud?

Asking these kinds of questions helps us think about mathematized read-alouds in a thoughtful and reflective way. This kind of thinking helps us acknowledge our successes and identify what we might work on next to strengthen our instructional practice and engage in learning with educators.

How can our PLC deepen as a community through our work with mathematizing?

Within the cycle of working as a PLC, it can be powerful to explicitly attend to how our community is deepening through this work together. Just as we want to build in time to reflect on what children are learning, we want to build in time to reflect on what we are learning and how we are growing as a community of educators. We can study who we are now and who we are becoming through this work. The unit of study becomes us!

Questions to guide PLC self-reflection include the following:

- How are we growing as a team of educators as we study mathematizing together?

- What are we learning, and what might be challenging for us?

- What is at the edge of our learning (content, complex practices in teaching, etc.)?

- What would it look like to map out our learning goals over time?

You may want to co-develop and revisit norms that support your work as a learning community. The following chart offers some professional norms that we learned from

Teacher Education by Design (TEDD.org, n.d). You may consider these norms as a launching point in developing your group norms. A big idea to remember is that through stories, we can work on complex aspects of teaching together as educators.

Professional Norms for Our Work Together

- Be willing to take risks with new ideas.
- Listen actively and generously.
- Build on others' ideas and invite others to participate.
- Give each other time to think and process ideas.
- Share ideas-in-progress and revise your thinking.
- Use specific language to describe what you see students doing, rather than labeling students. Avoid labels such as "low" and "high."
- Meet learners where they are (colleagues and students).

In sum, we have found that collaboratively planning for mathematizing read-aloud experiences with colleagues within a range of PLC structures is a powerful opportunity to deepen our own, and our collective, knowledge and hone instructional skills. Ongoing PLC work helps create lasting change and has the power to impact student and educator learning school-wide. Through mathematizing literature, PLCs can deepen knowledge of teaching and learning as well as study complex practices that educators enact. We find joy and wonder working together with colleagues to learn and grow our own teaching knowledge and practices; we hope you will, too!

Chapter 8
Family and Community Connections

I always want to move away from learning as a series of transactional experiences and toward learning as a way to elevate the agency of children, families, and communities. When a learning community comes together in mutual power, curiosity can then be free.
—Rekha Kuver, Public Library Youth and Family Services Manager

Stories carry across the contexts of a child's life. From home to an after-school program, from childcare to a relative's house, from a public library to preschool, from kindergarten into the elementary grades. In each of these spaces, a child often has access to stories, and the adults in their lives are often excited about reading and sharing stories with them. In this culminating chapter, we want to think about building family and community connections through mathematizing children's literature. What might it look like to build connections between the formal and informal learning settings of a child's life? What if stories were centered in those connections?

The Power of Familiarity

Listening to stories is a comfortable and familiar routine in a child's life. Children hear words, see illustrations, ask questions, and share ideas. This familiarity allows children to explore ideas and to be playful. Instead of learning how to be, a child can dive into a reading experience and think in creative ways.

I (Allison) recently saw the power of familiarity when visiting a school with my eleven-year-old daughter, Grace, who will be going to middle school next year. The students visiting the new school setting were invited to engage in a number talk around Christopher Danielson's mathematical routine, Which One Doesn't Belong? In this purposefully ambiguous and open-ended activity, mathematicians view four things (it may be numbers or objects) and are asked which one doesn't belong. There is no right answer; instead the power lies in inviting someone to argue for which item they believe does not belong with the others and why. As a set of four numbers was displayed, visitors were asked to turn and talk with a neighbor to say which number they believed did not belong. I observed Grace scoot forward in her chair. She repositioned her body to sit up on her legs, stretched her neck to see the numbers more clearly, and started talking. She had ideas to share! Grace described why each number could be the one that did not belong. She smiled, saying, "We do this at my school!" The familiarity drew her into the experience. A bridge was built from one part of her life to another, and it was empowering to her to draw upon ways of thinking like a mathematician in her current school to imagine thinking like a mathematician in a new setting.

Similar to the way the instructional routine of *Which One Doesn't Belong?* carries across settings, stories also carry across settings. Let's think about what it could look like for the network of educators in children's lives (spanning parents, caregivers, childcare and preschool providers, prekindergarten teachers, and librarians) to partner and leverage the familiarity of stories to explore mathematical ideas, and engage young mathematicians, in engaging ways.

How might I partner with families to learn together?

Stories, both oral and written, lie at the heart of families. Oral stories are often passed down from generation to generation. Favorite picture books may be well worn from being read over and over across the years. There are many ways families engage in storytelling in their lives. Creating an opening to know and hear families' stories in our classrooms allows us to understand more about our students. Perhaps families in your learning community can share stories that are important in their lives and expand our awareness of our students' experiences outside of school. Although we focus on printed children's literature in this book, it is worth exploring how families may have oral stories in their lives, how those stories are mathematical, and how those stories are a context for thinking like mathematicians. We believe that exploring storytelling has great potential!

When we think about learning with families flowing from home to school contexts, not just from school to home, we build bridges for better understanding the children we learn with each day and the knowledge they bring from home communities to our learning communities. We work to more clearly position families as knowing contributors. For example, in the story *A Different Pond* (Phi 2017), we join a boy and his father on an early morning fishing trip. Along the way we learn details about this family's life—the father's past in Vietnam and the loss of his brother in the war, the family's hard work to provide for their children as immigrants in a new land where everything is expensive, the boy's determined efforts to be helpful to his father. We see their resilience and determination as they return home with fish, knowing the family will eat well that evening. When reading this story with children, we learn about this family's values, history, and persistent way of being resilient in daily life. Being resilient and persevering is also a mathematical way of being.

We ask, as we explore children's literature, how can stories help us honor and build upon families' knowledge and cultural ways of being mathematical? How can stories elevate the agency of families (as Rekha Kuver eloquently states in her quote at the beginning of this chapter)? How might we invite families to share their own stories of resiliency and perseverance? What other mathematical ways of knowing and being can we recognize and explore in stories? How can we learn *from* and *with* families in more meaningful ways?

As we learn from the knowledge students and families bring to our school communities through their everyday cultural, linguistic, and mathematical ways of being, we must work to recognize the strengths and resources families hold (González, Moll, and Amanti 2005). For example, in *A Different Pond*, when we see the deep knowledge of perseverance that families have from their lived experiences, we pause to examine perseverance. When is perseverance recognized and valued as a strength and a resource that families bring to our learning communities? How must we rehumanize learning so that children and families who know how to persevere in life may persevere academically and intellectually within more inspiring and equitable schooling?

How might I share mathematizing ideas and tools with families?

Sharing the ways you're approaching stories as mathematicians within the classroom can deepen or perhaps spark new practices of reading and sharing stories at home. We encourage you to share what you're learning with children's families by inviting parents and caregivers to engage, alongside their child, in read-alouds during the school day or at evening events where you mathematize children's literature and stories together.

The questions as refrain (Appendix B) may also be a friendly place to begin. These open-ended questions can create an easy way for the adults in children's lives to begin approaching stories from a notice and wonder perspective. These questions are accessible and focus discussion of stories on a child's ideas and sense making, while also working to broaden perceptions of what counts as meaningful mathematics.

If you have time and resources, you might consider creating toolkits to send home to share with families. For example, you could gather supplies such as a few books for families to explore, the questions as refrain bookmark copied on cardstock, and a sketched-in guide that goes with the stories you've included that suggests stopping points and questions for exploring the books from Story Explore and Math Lens perspectives. The toolkit might also include some simple materials for Story Explore and Math Lens idea investigations such as counters, plastic cups, blank paper, and crayons (think back to Chapter 6 with Ms. Hadreas and Ms. Burris as they thought of idea investigations for their students). We would also include a laminated list of all the supplies in the kit and a short cover letter (in several languages, if possible) that welcomes a family to the kit and helps them know how to dig in. Figure 8.1 shows a sample cover letter.

Dear Families and Caregivers,

In our classroom, we are exploring stories as mathematicians! As we enjoy stories together, we notice and wonder about the mathematics in the story and in the illustrations. Although stories are often thought of as a wonderful way to support young readers and writers, we are learning that stories are also a way to grow as young mathematicians.

For example, in our classroom this week, we shared the story *Last Stop on Market Street* by Matt de la Peña. While reading this story, students noticed that the main characters, CJ and Nana, meet many people along a bus ride. Students wondered, "How many people did CJ meet?" As I listened to students count people as we reread the story, I learned that students are counting by ones and by twos. I could also hear they are starting to understand strategies for seeing quantities in small groups and counting on! Hearing students' ideas will help me plan for upcoming lessons, where we will continue to develop an understanding of counting strategies and the theme of community.

I encourage you to experiment with "mathematizing" stories at home! In this toolkit you'll find a few stories and accompanying suggestions for questions you may ask while enjoying these stories as mathematicians and readers. You'll also find some materials to continue exploring ideas after reading! The toolkit also contains a *questions as refrain* bookmark with sample questions you can use when reading any story with your child.

Beyond the books in this toolkit, we can explore almost any story with a mathematical lens! Remember math is all around us in our world! Have fun seeking out opportunities to find joy and wonder for math in stories you enjoy with your child.

Figure 8.1
A Sample Letter to Families and Caregivers

How might I partner with children's librarians to learn together?

Children's librarians hold tremendous knowledge of stories. They have stacks of books at their fingertips and are experts in knowing details of every story on the shelf. Have you ever had the experience of talking with a librarian, describing what you need, and as she listens, she says, "I have just the book for you!" She then walks over, bends down, runs her finger along the spines, and pulls out a story. Librarians know stories! We can all learn a lot from their expertise.

Whether working in a public library or an elementary school setting, children's librarians are excellent learning partners in mathematizing literature. We have learned a great deal through our collaborations with children's librarian Mie-Mie Wu. You'll remember Mie-Mie from her ideas about selecting stories in Chapter 3. She plans and facilitates family story time for children ages one to ten. For very young children, she may be the child's first teacher beyond family members. For the child's parents and caregivers, she may serve as their partner in learning how to read to and with children.

School librarians have the advantage of seeing groups of children on a regular basis, typically every week. These knowledgeable educators have the potential to help children make mathematical connections through Open Notice and Wonder reads and/or prompts as part of their regular story time routines, as well as enacting Math Lens reads of text-dependent or idea-enhancing new and interesting titles! We have found that children's librarians can seamlessly add mathematizing read-alouds and related prompts to their existing routines with great enthusiasm and success, making it an engaging way to extend mathematizing children's literature beyond the classroom. Additionally, school librarians may be an important member of the PLC learning in your context.

How can we partner with childcare, preschool, and prekindergarten providers?

Before arriving in elementary school classrooms, many children have spent time learning in childcare, preschool, and prekindergarten spaces. However, we rarely extend connections between these contexts of a child's early years and their learning experiences in elementary school and beyond. Stories hold tremendous power to build bridges between educational settings.

In our work we have collaborated with preschool teachers and childcare providers; their knowledge of child development and early learning pairs well with our mathematizing emphasis on noticing and wondering and exploring and discussing ideas. Stories are a common thread weaving together children's experiences across settings, and early childhood educators understand the power and value of using stories to explore complex concepts with young learners. As with older children, the context of a story provides rich opportunities for children to explore an idea from different perspectives and to relate the story to their own lives—with exciting results! In a community preschool we had the opportunity to work alongside a group of teachers to collaboratively plan and enact an Open Notice and Wonder read of *The Most Magnificent Thing* (Spires 2014) with a group of four- and five-year-old children. The teachers had insightful observations and thoughts about how to bring this story to life in dynamic ways, such as reenacting the moment the girl's finger gets pinched and talking about what it must be like to have swirls of frustration overhead! The children delighted everyone with creative ideas of what they noticed and wondered about from the story, including why the illustrator chose to leave the background black and white and how to make something magnificent by drawing lots and lots of hearts on it!

We also worked with a Mandarin-English bilingual preschool class to mathematize stories across languages. Familiar with a range of narrative structures, the teacher of this class showed us how to tell a story in a way that draws on children's experiences and to narrate a children's book in two languages rather than reading it outright—an experience that led to hands-on activities and children's sharing of their own stories, all facilitated by this fantastic teacher. These experiences with early childhood educators helped us see the power of using stories to build bridges between preschool and kindergarten.

Stories allow all of us to think about and make sense of our own lives while also giving us insights into the lives of others and to the world around us. Within stories, we change the way we see our lives, communities, and world. Practicing seeing mathematics within a story allows children and teachers to look up from the pages and notice mathematics in more vibrant ways in the world around us. Practicing thinking like a mathematician within a story opens up opportunities to think like a mathematician in our everyday lives. Practicing using mathematics to make sense of a story helps us see, and remember, that we can use mathematics to make sense of our world. Thinking as a mathematician becomes a way of being, and this enriches our lives.

A Last Word

Thank you for thinking about the ideas in this book with us. Writing them for you gave us the gift of learning and a welcome opportunity to shift, revise, deepen, and grow our thinking. We hope you will playfully experiment with mathematizing a favorite book you love or explore a story that is excitingly new to you. We know you will innovate with the ideas and generate new and powerful ways for children, yourself, families, and communities to experience joy and wonder for mathematics through stories.

Appendices

APPENDIX A:
Open Notice and Wonder Planning Template

OPEN NOTICE AND WONDER

Book Title and Author

○ **Read and enjoy the story.**
As teacher and reader, what do I notice? What do I wonder?

○ **Anticipate and mark intended places for pausing the story.**
What do I anticipate will be interesting or curious to my students?
Where do I anticipate pausing to invite students to share? Why?
Place sticky note on the pages.

○ **Plan for story launch.**
With my stopping points in mind, how will I introduce the story using the cover? What might students notice and wonder on the cover?

○ **Gather chart paper and different-colored markers.**

APPENDIX B:
Questions as Refrain Bookmark

**GUIDING
QUESTIONS**
Questions as Refrain

 MATH

- What do you see, notice, or wonder about?

- What (numbers, combinations, patterns, shapes, other math concept) do you see?

- How might you use the illustrations to show your thinking?

 LITERACY

- What do you think will happen in this story, and why do you think so?

- What will happen next? How do you know?

- What connections can you make between this story and another story or something else you know?

Mathematizing Children's Literature: Sparking Connections, Joy, and Wonder Through Read-Alouds and Discussion by Allison Hintz and Antony T. Smith. Copyright © 2022. Stenhouse Publishers.

APPENDIX C:
Focused Read Planning Template

FOCUSED READ

Book Title and Author

Discussion Structure	**Order of Read**
○ Story Explore	○ 2nd read
○ Math Lens	○ 3rd read
	○ Other

Making Connections
Which ideas from the first Open Notice and Wonder read (and/or the Story Explore or Math Lens read) do I want to pursue? Why?

What portion of the story will I reread?

○ Entire story
○ Part of the story
○ Revisit illustration(s)

Where Might We Pause and Why?

Page (Description)	Story Explore or Math Lens Question/Prompt

How Will I Launch the Story?

APPENDIX D:
Idea Investigation Planning Template

IDEA INVESTIGATION

Book Title and Author

Idea Investigation (Discussing, Drawing, Writing)
What interactive experience will extend the mathematical and/or literary thinking?

Which read-aloud discussion(s) does this investigation extend?

○ Math Lens
○ Story Explore
○ Integrated Math Lens and Story Explore

How does the investigation build on and deepen children's ideas about the math and/or literacy in the story and our discussions of the story?

How will I launch the investigation?

Materials
What materials do we need?

Sharing Out Thinking, Ideas, and Work

When and how will students share their work?

○ As they work
○ After they work
○ Whole group
○ Small groups

What will I listen to/for or notice about students' work?

APPENDIX E:
Listening to Students at Work Note-Taking Form

Strategy	Students' Thinking	Students	Order for Sharing

PROFESSIONAL RESOURCES AND REFERENCES

Aguirre, Julia, Karen Mayfield-Ingram, and Danny Martin. 2013. *The Impact of Identity in K–8 Mathematics Learning and Teaching: Rethinking Equity-Based Practices.* Reston, VA: National Council of Teachers of Mathematics.

Beck, Isabel, and Margaret McKeown. 2001. "Text Talk: Capturing the Benefits of Read-Aloud Experiences for Young Children." *The Reading Teacher* 55: 10–20.

Bishop, Rudine Sims. 1990. "Mirrors, Windows, and Sliding Glass Doors." *Perspectives: Choosing and Using Books for the Classroom* 6 (3): ix–xi.

Carpenter, Thomas. 1999. *Children's Mathematics: Cognitively Guided Instruction.* Portsmouth, NH: Heinemann.

Carpenter, Thomas, Elizabeth Fennema, Megan Franke, Linda Levi, and Susan Empson. 2015. *Children's Mathematics: Cognitively Guided Instruction.* 2nd ed. Portsmouth, NH: Heinemann.

Cazden, Courtney. 2001. *Classroom Discourse: The Language of Teaching and Learning.* 2nd ed. Portsmouth, NH: Heinemann.

Chapin, Suzanne, Mary O'Connor, and Nancy Anderson. 2009. *Classroom Discussions: Using Math Talk to Help Students Learn, Grades K–6.* 2nd ed. Sausalito, CA: Math Solutions.

Codell, Esmé. 2003. *How to Get Your Child to Love Reading.* Chapel Hill, NC: Algonquin Books.

Common Core State Standards Initiative. 2011. *Common Core State Standards for English Language Arts and Mathematics.* http://www.corestandards.org/the-standards.

Duffy, Gerald. 2004. "Teachers Who Improve Reading Achievement: What Research Says About What They Do and How to Develop Them." In *Improving Reading Achievement Through Professional Development*, ed. Dorothy Strickland and Michael Kamil. Norwood, MA: Christopher Gordon.

Fisher, Douglas, James Flood, Diane Lapp, and Nancy Frey. 2004. "Interactive Read-Alouds: Is There a Common Set of Implementation Practices?" *The Reading Teacher* 58: 8–17.

Fosnot, Catherine, and Maarten Dolk. 2001. *Young Mathematicians at Work. Constructing Number Sense, Addition, and Subtraction.* Portsmouth, NH: Heinemann.

González, Norma, Luis Moll, and Cathy Amanti. 2005. *Funds of Knowledge: Theorizing Practices in Households, Communities, and Classrooms.* Mahwah, NJ: Erlbaum.

Graves, Michael, Connie Juel, Bonnie Graves, and Peter Dewitz. 2011. *Teaching Reading in the 21st Century: Motivating All Learners.* 5th ed. New York: Pearson.

Gutiérrez, R. 2018. *Rehumanizing Mathematics for Black, Indigenous, and Latinx Students.* Annual Perspectives in Mathematics Education, vol. 2018. Reston, VA: National Council of Teachers of Mathematics.

Hord, Shirley. 1997. *Professional Learning Communities: Communities of Continuous Inquiry and Improvement.* Austin, TX: Southwest Educational Development Laboratory.

Joyce, Bruce, and Beverly Showers. 1980. "Improving Inservice Training: The Messages of Research." *Educational Leadership* 37: 379–385.

Kazemi, Elham, and Allison Hintz. 2014. *Intentional Talk: How to Structure and Lead Productive Mathematical Discussions.* Portland, ME: Stenhouse.

Layne, Steven. 2015. *In Defense of Read-Aloud: Sustaining Best Practice.* Portland, ME: Stenhouse.

Lieberman, Ann, and Lynn Miller. 1999. *Teachers: Transforming Their World and Their Work.* Alexandria, VA: Association for Supervision and Curriculum Development.

Meier, Deborah. 1995. *The Power of Their Ideas: Lessons for America from a Small School in Harlem.* Boston: Beacon.

Moje, Elizabeth. 2007. "Developing Socially Just Subject-Matter Instruction: A Review of the Literature on Disciplinary Literacy Teaching. *Review of Research in Education* 31: 1–44.

National Council of Teachers of Mathematics. 2014. *Principles to Actions: Ensuring Mathematical Success for All.* Reston, VA: National Council of Teachers of Mathematics.

Nichols, Maria. 2006. *Comprehension Through Conversation: The Power of Purposeful Talk in the Reading Workshop.* Portsmouth, NH: Heinemann.

Routman, Regie. 2003. *Reading Essentials: The Specifics You Need to Teach Reading Well.* Portsmouth, NH: Heinemann.

Serafini, Frank, and Lindsey Moses. 2014. "The Roles of Children's Literature in the Primary Grades." *The Reading Teacher* 67: 465–468.

Showers, Beverly, and Bruce Joyce. 1996. "The Evolution of Peer Coaching." *Educational Leadership* 53: 12-16.

Sipe, Lawrence. 2000. "The Construction of Literary Understanding by First and Second Graders in Oral Response to Picture Storybook Read-Alouds." *Reading Research Quarterly* 35: 252–275.

———. 2002. "Talking Back and Taking Over: Young Children's Expressive Engagement During Storybook Read-Alouds." *The Reading Teacher* 55: 476–483.

Smith, Margaret, and Mary Kay Stein. 2011. *5 Practices for Orchestrating Productive Math Discussions.* Reston, VA: National Council of Teachers of Mathematics.

TEDD | teacher education by design. https://tedd.org/the-design. (n.d). https://tedd.org/.

Trelease, Jim. 2013. *The Read-Aloud Handbook.* 7th ed. New York: Penguin.

Tyson, Kersti. 2011. *Listening Matters: Developing Listening Spectra for Engaging Education.* University of Washington.

Warshauer, Hiroko. 2014. "Productive Struggle in Middle School Mathematics Classrooms." *Journal of Mathematics Teacher Education* 18: 375–400.

CHILDREN'S LITERATURE BIBLIOGRAPHY

Allen, Pamela. 1983. *Who Sank the Boat?* New York: Coward-McCann.

Baker, Keith. 1999. *Quack and Count.* San Diego: Harcourt Brace.

Barton, Byron. 2014. *My Bus.* New York: Greenwillow Books.

Bingham, Kelly. 2014. *Circle Square Moose.* Illustrated by Paul O. Zelinsky. New York: Greenwillow Books.

Boyd, Lizi. 2014. *Flashlight.* San Francisco: Chronicle Books.

Burns, Marilyn. 1994. *The Greedy Triangle.* Illustrated by Gordon Silveria. New York: Scholastic.

Carle, Eric. 1969. *The Very Hungry Caterpillar.* Cleveland, OH: Collins-World.

Cornwall, Gaia. 2017. *Jabari Jumps.* Somerville, MA: Candlewick.

Cousins, Lucy. 2017. *Hooray for Fish.* Somerville, MA: Candlewick.

de la Peña, Matt. 2015. *Last Stop on Market Street.* Illustrated by C. Robinson. New York: G.P. Putnam's Sons.

Dodd, Emma. 2003. *Dog's Colorful Day: A Messy Story About Colors and Counting.* New York: Dutton Children's Books.

Dodds, Dayle Ann. 2009. *Full House : An Invitation to Fractions.* Illustrated by Abby Carter. Cambridge, MA: Candlewick.

Ghahremani, Susie. 2018. *Stack the Cats.* New York: Abrams Appleseed.

Giganti, Paul. 1999. *Each Orange Had 8 Slices : A Counting Book.* Illustrated by Donald Crews. New York: Greenwillow Books.

Jeffers, Oliver. 2011. *Stuck.* New York: Philomel Books.

Jenkins, Emily. 2011. *Small Medium Large.* Illustrated by Tomek Bogacki. Cambridge, MA: Star Bright.

Jonas, Ann. 1997. *Splash!* New York: Greenwillow Books.

Juster, Norton. 1961. *The Phantom Tollbooth.* Illustrated by Jules Feiffer. New York: Alfred A. Knopf.

Keats, Ezra Jack. 1976. *The Snowy Day.* New York: Viking.

Litwin, Eric. 2012. *Pete the Cat and His Four Groovy Buttons.* Illustrated by James Dean. New York: Harper.

Mader, C. Roger. 2014. *Tip Top Cat.* New York: Houghton Mifflin Harcourt.

McElligott, Matthew. 2012. *The Lion's Share: A Tale of Halving Cake and Eating It Too.* New York: Bloomsbury USA Childrens.

Murray, Diana. 2016. *City Shapes.* Illustrated by Bryan Collier. New York: Little, Brown and Company.

Pfister, Marcus. 1992. *The Rainbow Fish*. Illustrated by J. Alison James. New York: North-South Books.

Phi, Bao. 2017. *A Different Pond*. Illustrated by Thi Bui. North Mankato, MN: Capstone Young Readers.

Sayre, April Pulley, and Jeff Sayre. 2006. *One Is a Snail, Ten Is a Crab: A Counting by Feet Book*. Illustrated by Randy Cecil. Cambridge, MA: Candlewick.

Schoonmaker, Elizabeth. 2011. *Square Cat*. New York: Aladdin.

Spires, Ashley. 2014. *The Most Magnificent Thing*. Illustrated by Yasemin Ucar. Toronto, ON: Kids Can Press.

Stanton, Beck, and Matt Stanton. 2017. *This Is a Ball*. New York: Little, Brown Books for Young Readers.

Tankard, Jeremy. 2007. *Grumpy Bird*. New York: Scholastic.

Thong, Roseanne. 2015. *Round Is a Tortilla : A Book of Shapes*. Illustrated by John Parra. San Francisco: Chronicle Books.

Willems, Mo. 2007. *There Is a Bird on Your Head*. New York: Hyperion.

INDEX

Page numbers followed by *f* indicate figures.

A

adaptive teaching, 175–176
artifacts
    planning, 118
    reflecting on and learning from, 176–177
assessment, formative, opportunities for, 25

B

bilingual mathematizing, 187
book selection
    collaborative, 156, 157, 158
    different approaches to, 39–44
    engaging story as basis for, 42–44
    importance of, 6
    mathematizing step, as, 26
    Open Notice and Wonder and, 47, 61
    overview, 39
    read-aloud characteristics for, 30–32
    reasons for, 39, 42, 44
    reflection and discussion questions on, 44
    sequencing, 174
    specific mathematical concepts as basis for, 39–42
    text types for, 4, 32–39
book types. *See also* idea-enhancing books; illustration-exploring books; text-dependent books
    benefits across, 39
    described, 32–38
    key learnings around, 38
    overlapping of, 32, 33

C

charting/charts
    additional Idea Investigations, 171, 177
    collaborative planning, 156, 157
    focused approach to, 40*f*, 41*f*
    Integrated Idea Investigation, 125–126, 128*f*, 130, 131
    Math Lens, 102, 106–108
    Math Lens Idea Investigation, 122–123, 124, 125*f*
    open approach to, 42–43
    Open Notice and Wonder, 49, 50*f*, 51, 54, 58, 58–59, 63, 74, 83, 96
    reflecting on and learning from, 177
    Story Explore, 79, 83, 102
    Story Explore Idea Investigation, 114
childcare providers, partnering with, 186–187
Circle Square Moose (Bingham), 95
City Shapes (Murray), 10, 55–57, 145–146
Codell, Esme Raji, 30
Cognitively Guided Instruction (CGI), 19
collaboration, cross-disciplinary, 3, 4, 25, 27
collaborative planning. *See also* professional learning communities (PLCs)
    Idea Investigations, 145, 146, 171–172
    steps for, 157
    supporting, 11
    vignette, 156–158
commitments
    addressing, 18, 20, 23–24, 26, 27
    exploring, 6–11
    list of, 5
    vision across, 11–12
communities
    building connections with, 182
    partnering with, 183, 186–187
communities, learning. *See* professional learning communities (PLCs)
complex teaching practices, planning for and enacting, 166–172
Comprehension Through Conversation (Nichols), 66
connections, making, 3
    deepening knowledge by, 164
    encouraging, 10, 24
    family and community, 182–187
    focused reads, 90
    Idea Investigations, 112, 113, 115, 116, 136, 151
    Math Lens, 80, 83, 92–94, 103
    planning for, 92–94, 94–95, 96
    Story Explore, 71, 74, 76, 78, 79, 94–95, 96, 97–98

counting books, 35
Counting Collections, 84
cross-disciplinary collaboration, 3, 4, 25, 27
culture, listening, 8
curiosity. *See also* noticing and wondering
    fostering, 5, 6, 7, 16
    mathematizing bringing, 39

D
Danielson, Christopher, 182
decision-making, in-the-moment, 175, 176
Different Pond, A (Phi), 183, 184
disciplinary literacy, 25
discussions
    benefits from, 2–3, 9, 24
    emphasizing, 10
    encouraging, 23
    engaging in, 4
    facilitating, 6
    importance of, 8–9
    integrating math and literacy through, 25
    promoting, 2
discussion structure, selecting, 90
diverse literature, commitment to, 7
Dog's Colorful Day (Dodd), 35, 94, 142–144
drawings
    additional Idea Investigations and, 142–144,
        145, 150
    Math Lens Idea Investigation, 123–124
    Story Explore Idea Investigation, 115, 119, 120*f*

E
Each Orange Had 8 slices: A Counting Book
    (Giganti), 3
everyday lives, making connections to, 10

F
familiarity, power of, 182
families
    building connections with, 182
    cover letter to, 184, 185*f*
    partnering with, 183–184
    sharing toolkits with, 184
Fetter, Annie, 46
first grade
    additional Idea Investigations, 137, 142–144,
        145–146, 149–150
    collaborative planning, 156–158
    Math Lens, 70, 80–90, 113
    Math Lens Idea Investigation, 119–125
    Open Notice and Wonder, 47–54, 70
    productive struggle and, 170–171
    Story Explore, 70, 71–79, 113, 175–176
    Story Explore Idea Investigation, 113–115
first read, focus for, 55
Flashlight (Boyd), 6, 37–38, 164–165
flexibility, 26, 91, 96, 173, 174
focal story, co-selecting, 157, 158
focus
    limiting story ideas or topics for, 94, 95
    maintaining mathematic, 94
focused reads. *See also* Math Lens; Story
    Explore
    guiding questions for, 66
    planning, 71, 90–91
    planning template for, 72–73*f*, 80–81*f*, 90*f*, 91
    purpose of, 70
    read order for, 96–97
    structures for, 70
formative assessment, opportunities for, 25
Full House (Dodds), 34, 138–139, 161, 177

G
Greedy Triangle, The (Burns), 3
Grumpy Bird (Tankard), 33, 94, 164

H
Hooray for Fish (Cousins), 37, 177
How to Get Your Child to Love Reading (Codell), 30

I
idea-enhancing books, 33, 35–36, 42, 47, 152, 186
Idea Investigations. *See also* Integrated Idea
    Investigation; Math Lens Idea Investigation;
    Story Explore Idea Investigation
    activities not intended for, 118
    additional suggestions and examples,
        136–152, 171–172, 177
    benefits from, 152
    collaboratively planning, 145, 146, 171–172
    described, 112
    mathematizing step, as, 26–27

noting to follow up with, 79, 89, 90, 102, 109
planning, 116–119
planning templates, 116, 117*f*, 118, 171
powerful, 118
reflection and discussion questions on, 152–153
ideas
    encouraging, 6, 9
    focus on, 4–5
    listening to, 2, 4, 6, 8–9, 10
ideas, capturing. *See* charting/charts
illustration-exploring books, 33, 36–38, 42, 177
In Defense of Read-Aloud (Layne), 30
inferences, using, supporting, 24
Initiate-Respond-Evaluate (IRE) patterns, moving beyond, 8
instructional coaches, 3, 156, 158, 159, 168
Integrated Idea Investigation
    planning, 112, 125–126
    planning template, 125, 126–127*f*
    third grade, 112, 113, 125–136
    vignette, 128–136
interactive read-alouds. *See also* Math Lens; Open Notice and Wonder; Story Explore
    benefits of, 23–25
    described, 2, 23
    elements of, 23
    enriching, 10
    mathematizing step, as, 26
investigation launch
    Integrated Idea Investigation, 128
    Math Lens Idea Investigation, 122
    planning, 116
    Story Explore Idea Investigation, 114–115

J

Jabari Jumps (Cornwall), 2, 4, 7, 10, 16–18, 20, 24, 36, 94, 150–152
joy and wonder, fostering, 2, 4, 6, 8, 39, 179, 187

K

kindergarten, Idea Investigations, 137, 140, 145–146

L

language development, supporting, 10

Last Stop on Market Street (de la Peña), 4, 164
    connections to everyday lives in, 10
    focused readings of, 70, 96
    Math Lens, 70, 80–90, 91, 94
    Math Lens Idea Investigation, 119–125
    Open Notice and Wonder, 47–54, 60*f*, 70
    read order for, 96, 173
    sequencing span, 173
    Story Explore, 70, 71–79, 91, 175–176
    Story Explore Idea Investigation, 113–115
Layne, Steven, 30
learning and teaching. *See* teaching and learning
learning communities. *See* professional learning communities (PLCs)
librarians, 3, 4, 30, 186
Lion's Share, The (McElligott)
    focused approach to, 41
    Integrated Idea Investigation, 125–136
    Math Lens, 103–109, 112, 113
    Open Notice and Wonder, 61–65
    read order for, 96, 173
    sequencing span, 173
    Story Explore, 97–102, 112, 113
listening, 2, 4, 6, 8–9, 10
listening culture, 8
literacy and math integration, encouraging, 25, 27
literacy instruction, essential part of, 2
literacy skills, opportunities for assessing, 25
literary-focused read. *See* Story Explore
literary style, 31, 47
literature. *See also specific children's book titles*
    exploring mathematics through, described, 2–4, 5
    multicultural/diverse, commitment to, 7

M

materials
    additional Idea Investigations, 142, 145, 171
    collaborative planning, 156
    Idea Investigation, 118, 119, 139
    Integrated Idea Investigation, 128
    Math Lens, 85
    Math Lens Idea Investigation, 123, 184
    Open Notice and Wonder, 58, 61

Story Explore Idea Investigation, 115
mathematical agency
    actualizing, 87, 125
    empowering, 42
    nurturing and affirming, 21–22
mathematical context, 7
mathematical identity
    defined, 21
    development of, 3
    focus on, 4–5, 16
    nurturing and affirming, 19, 21, 22
mathematical thinking
    complexity of, 7
    empowering, 9
    recognizing and celebrating, 19
mathematics
    rehumanizing, 11–12, 21, 22
mathematics and literacy instruction
    exploring connections between, 3
    integrating, 4
mathematizing
    defined, 3
    described, 18
    process steps, 26–27
math-focused read. *See* Math Lens
Math Lens, 25, 173
    adapting plans and, 174
    described, 70
    different read order for, 97
    evolution of ideas and, 119
    first grade, 70, 80–90, 113
    integrating ideas from Story Explore and, 112,
        113, 116
    interactive read-aloud, as, 26
    librarian story time and, 186
    planning, 70, 80, 90, 91, 103
    planning essentials, 92–94
    planning templates, 80–81*f*, 103–104*f*
    selecting ideas from, 97, 112, 113, 116
    third grade, 103–109, 112, 113
    time for, 173
    toolkit for families, 184
    unexpected moments and, 175
    vignettes, 83–90, 96, 104–109
Math Lens Idea Investigation. *See also* Integrated
    Idea Investigation

first grade, 119–125
    planning, 119
    planning templates, 119, 120–121*f*
    toolkit for families, 184
    vignette, 122–125
"mathy" books. *See* text-dependent books
Most Magnificent Thing, The (Spires), 10, 95, 97,
    162, 164, 168, 187
multicultural literature, commitment to, 7
My Bus (Barton), 144–145

N

narrative pacing, 31, 47
National Council of Teachers of Mathematics, 169
Nichols, Maria, 66
note taking, 48, 79, 80, 91, 109, 112, 116, 125,
    134, 146
note taking form, 134, 135*f*
noticing, described, 49
noticing and wondering. *See also* Math Lens;
    Open Notice and Wonder; Story Explore
    anticipating, 57–58
    book types and, 33
    celebrating, 2, 6, 7
    delving into, 16–18, 20
    educators engaging in, 3, 4, 55–57, 61, 156–157
    focused approach to, 39–42
    inspiration for, 46
    open approach to, 42–44
    playful space for, 7–8
    questions for going beyond, 66–67
    repeated practice of, 46

O

One Is a Snail, Ten Is a Crab (Sayre and Sayre),
    92–93, 141–142
Open Notice and Wonder, 25, 158, 159, 173
    adapting plans and, 51, 52, 57–58, 174
    described, 47
    different read order for, 97
    evolution of ideas from, 112, 119
    first grade, 47–54, 70
    guiding questions for, 66–67
    interactive read-aloud, as, 26
    librarian story time and, 186
    planning, 49, 50*f*, 55–58, 61, 187

planning templates, 59, 60*f*, 61–62*f*
reflection and discussion questions on, 67
selecting ideas from, 70, 74, 83, 90, 92, 96, 97, 103, 116
third grade, 61–65
unexpected moments and, 175
vignettes, 47–49, 50–54, 62–65, 96
oral stories, 183

P

partnering
    community, 183, 186–187
    family, 183–184
Pete the Cat and His Four Groovy Buttons (Litwin), 4
Phantom Tollbooth, The (Juster), 19–20
planning. *See also* collaborative planning
    adaptive, 51, 52, 57–58, 174, 175, 176
    focused reads, 90–91
    Idea Investigations, 116–119
    Integrated Idea Investigation, 112, 125–126
    Math Lens, 70, 80, 90, 91, 103
    Math Lens Idea Investigation, 119
    Open Notice and Wonder, 49, 50*f*, 55–58, 61, 187
    Story Explore, 70, 71, 90, 91, 97–98
    Story Explore Idea Investigation, 115–116
planning essentials
    Math Lens, 92–94
    Story Explore, 94–96
planning templates
    collaborative, 157
    focused reads, 90, 91
    Idea Investigation, 116, 117*f*, 118, 171
    Integrated Idea Investigation, 125, 126–127*f*
    Math Lens, 80–81*f*, 103–104*f*
    Math Lens Idea Investigation, 119, 120–121*f*
    Open Notice and Wonder, 59, 60*f*, 61–62*f*
    Story Explore, 71, 72–73*f*, 97, 98–99*f*
    Story Explore Idea Investigation, 113–114*f*
planning time, 115, 119, 156–157, 173
planning tools, 158
playfulness

context for, 7, 8
    nurturing, 2
playful space, commitment to, 7–8
power, shifting, 6, 16, 21
predictions, using, supporting, 24
preschool teachers, partnering with, 186–187
Principles to Actions (National Council of Teachers of Mathematics), 169
problem solving
    Cognitively Guided Instruction and, 19
    mathematical life and, 18
    supporting, 9
productive struggle, engaging in, 11, 97, 167, 169–172
professional learning communities (PLCs). *See also* collaborative planning
    asking open-ended questions, 167–169
    benefits of ongoing work, 179
    central purpose of, 160
    common questions, 173–179
    common set of practices, 159
    co-planning vignette, 156–158
    deepening knowledge of literacy, 163–166
    deepening knowledge of math ideas/ concepts, 161–162
    deepening knowledge of math practices, 162–163
    described, 158
    enacting complex teaching practices, 166–172
    engaging in, 158–159
    learning through mathematizing, 160–166
    members, 159, 186
    self-reflection, 178–179
    structures and activities, 159–160
professional norms, 178–179
prompts. *See* questions/prompts

Q

Quack and Count (Baker), 39–41, 164, 174
questions as refrain
    bookmark, 66*f*, 67, 167, 184
    described, 66–67
    Math Lens opportunity for, 92
    professional learning communities and, 167
questions/prompts. *See also* stopping points

questions/prompts (cont.)
  collaborative planning, 156
  creating space for investigating, 21, 22
  encouraging, 46
  mathematics driven by, 18
  open-ended, 10, 11, 40, 66–67, 92,
    167–169, 170, 171
  planning, 96, 98
  providing opportunities for children to
    generate, 9, 20, 46
  targeted, 40, 79

R
Rainbow Fish, The (Pfister), 33
read-aloud extensions. See Idea Investigations
Read-Aloud Handbook, The (Trelease), 30
read-alouds. See also interactive read-alouds
  characteristics of, 30–32
  complexifying, 11
  reflecting on our own learning from,
    177–178
  trying different types of, 4
reading aloud
  benefits of, 22–23
  essential, as, 2
  expanding traditional view of, 2
  joyful, as, 2
  key features of, 10–11
reading development, supporting, 10
Reading Essentials (Routman), 22
read order, 26, 46–47, 51, 67, 70, 80, 90,
  96–97, 157, 158, 173
reads/rereads, choosing portion of story for,
  26, 61, 71, 75, 78, 83, 86, 88, 91, 97, 104
Round Is a Tortilla (Thong), 10, 146–148
Routman, Regie, 22

S
second grade, 21
  additional Idea Investigations, 144–145,
    146–148, 150–152, 171–172
  collaborative planning for, 171–172
  noticing and wondering vignette, 16–18
self-reflection, 178–179
sentence starters, 49, 50f
  Math Lens Idea Investigation, 122, 123, 124

planning for, 118
Sipe, Lawrence, 23–24
Small Medium Large (Jenkins), 95
Snowy Day, The (Keats), 36–37, 95, 149–150,
  167–168
Splash! (Jonas), 32–33, 140, 171–172
Square Cat (Schoonmaker), 34–35, 95, 96–97
Stack the Cats (Ghahremani), 94, 95f, 170–171, 174
sticky notes, using, 49, 57, 80, 82f, 91, 96, 98,
  105, 116, 156
stopping points
  adapting plans and, 174
  focused read, 91
  Math Lens, 86, 88, 89, 100, 101, 105, 106,
    184
  Open Notice and Wonder, 49, 50, 51,
    52–53, 57–58, 62, 64, 65
  Story Explore, 75, 76, 77, 78, 96, 98, 184
storyboard, 115–116
story context, 7–8
Story Explore, 25, 173
  adapting plans and, 174
  described, 70
  different read order for, 97
  evolution of ideas and, 119
  first grade, 70, 71–79, 113, 175–176
  integrating ideas from Math Lens and, 112,
    113, 116
  interactive read-aloud, as, 26
  planning, 70, 71, 90, 91, 97–98
  planning essentials, 94–96
  planning templates, 71, 72–73f, 97, 98–99f
  selecting ideas from, 80, 83, 92, 103, 112,
    113, 114, 116
  third grade, 97–102, 112
  time for, 173
  toolkit for families, 184
  unexpected moments and, 175
  vignettes, 74–79, 96, 99–102
Story Explore Idea Investigation. See also
  Integrated Idea Investigation
  evolution of ideas and, 119
  first grade, 113–115
  planning, 115–116
  planning templates, 113–114f
  selecting ideas from, 119

toolkit for families, 184

vignette, 114–115

story launch

Math Lens, 83, 99–100, 104

Open Notice and Wonder, 47–48, 62–64

planning for, 58, 61, 96

Story Explore, 74–75, 96

story problems

compared to story context, 7–8

differences between mathematizing stories and, 19–21

similarities between mathematizing stories and, 18–19

Stuck (Jeffers), 42–44

T

Teacher Education by Design, 179

teaching and learning. *See also* professional learning communities (PLCs)

commitments for, 4–12, 18, 20, 23–24, 26, 27

cross-disciplinary collaboration for, 3, 4, 25, 27

grounded in mathematical life, 18

invitation for, 13

shared principles and beliefs about, 18–19

supporting both, 11–12, 27

text-dependent books, 3–4, 7, 32–33, 34–35, 39–42, 61, 136, 138, 140, 142, 174, 186

There Is a Bird on Your Head (Willems), 4

third grade

additional Idea Investigations, 138–139, 141, 161, 177

Integrated Idea Investigation, 112, 113, 125–136

Math Lens, 103–109, 112, 113

Open Notice and Wonder, 61–65

Story Explore, 97–102, 112

This Is a Ball (Stanton and Stanton), 136–137, 162

Tip Top Cat (Mader), 10

toolkits, 184

Trelease, Jim, 30

U

unexpected moments, decision-making for, 175–176

V

Very Hungry Caterpillar, The (Carle), 35–36

visual interest, 31, 47, 61

vocabulary development, supporting, 10, 24

W

Which One Doesn't Belong? routine, 182

Who Sank the Boat (Allen), 164, 174, 175

wondering, described, 49. *See also* noticing and wondering

worksheets, contrast to, 112

Wu, Mie-Mie, 30, 32, 186

CREDITS

Figures 1.1 and 6.35, *Jabari Jumps*. Copyright © 2017 by Gaia Cornwall. Reproduced by permission of the publisher, Candlewick Press, Somerville, MA.

Figures 3.2 and 6.20, *Splash!* by Ann Jonas. Copyright © 1995 by Ann Jonas. Used by permission of HarperCollins Publishers.

Figures 3.3, 6.22, and 6.23, Excerpts and "Illustrations" from *Dog's Colorful Day: A Messy Story About Colors and Counting* by Emma Dodd, copyright © 2000 by Tucker Slingsby, Ltd. Used by permission of Dutton Children's Books, an imprint of Penguin Young Readers Group, a division of Penguin Random House LLC. All rights reserved.

Figure 3.4, Copyright © Eric Carle. Used with permission by Penguin Random House.

Figures 3.5 and 6.33, Copyright © Ezra Jack Keats. Used with permission by Penguin Random House.

Figures 3.6 and 7.3, *Hooray for Fish*. Copyright © 2005 by Lucy Cousins. Reproduced by permission of the publisher, Candlewick Press, Somerville, MA on behalf of Walker Books, London.

Figures 3.7 and 3.8, From *Flashlight* © 2014 by Lizi Boyd. Used with permission of Chronicle Books LLC, San Francisco. Visit ChronicleBooks.com.

Figure 3.11, Reprinted by permission of HarperCollins Publishers Ltd © 2011 Oliver Jeffers.

Figures 4.1, 4.2, 5.1, and 5.7, "Illustrations," by Christian Robinson, copyright © 2015 by Christian Robinson; and Excerpt(s) from *Last Stop on Market Street* by Matt de la Peña, text copyright © 2015 by Matt de la Peña. Used by permission of G.P. Putnam's Sons Books for Young Readers, an imprint of Penguin Young Readers Group, a division of Penguin Random House LLC. All rights reserved.